FOCAL CINEBOOKS

HOW TO MAKE FILMS AT SCHOOL
by J. D. Beal
casebound and paperback

HOW TO DO SOUND FILMS
by D. M. Neale and R. A. Hole

HOW TO FILM
by G. Wain

HOW TO EDIT
by H. Baddeley

HOW TO MAKE 8mm. FILMS
by N. Bau

HOW TO CARTOON
by J. Halas and B. Privett

HOW TO MAKE COLOUR FILMS
by C. L. Thomson

HOW TO TITLE
by L. F. Minter

HOW TO PLAN YOUR SUPER 8mm. FILMS
by C. V. Willson

HOW TO ANIMATE CUT-OUTS
by C. H. Barton

John Halas and Bob Privett

HOW TO CARTOON

for amateur films

Sixth Impression

FOCAL PRESS
London and New York

First published in 1951

Second Edition 1955

Third Edition 1958

Fourth Impression 1962

Fifth Impression 1970

Sixth Impression 1975

ISBN 0 240 44813 8

Published in Japanese by
Bijutsu Shuppan-sha, Tokyo

PRINTED AND MADE IN GREAT BRITAIN
BY FLETCHER AND SON LTD, NORWICH

Foreword

The fascination of making a static picture move is as deeply rooted in human nature as is the artistic instinct itself.

From as early as the fourteenth century, well before the discovery of films, many scientists and artists were intrigued by the problem of motion.

Before the live action film turned towards realism, both cartoon and live action had the same "magic" effect on the audience. Directors regarded them as means to reach into the supernatural.

The cartoon film is a true disciple of that very early film.

Its technique goes back to the Victorian "Wheel of Life". This gadget consisted of a small wheel inside a large one. Drawings of a galloping horseman in a number of positions were fixed on to the smaller inner wheel, and a hole cut in the larger outer one. By turning a handle attached to the smaller wheel and looking through the hole, the onlooker could watch what appeared to be a horse galloping along. An illusion of movement was created as the eye had no time to distinguish individual drawings, but could only see all of them as one producing a continuous flow of movement.

The basic principle of cartoon animation is still the same. The method of production has of course gone ahead, but the conception of creating an illusion of continuous motion by means of individual pictures remains unchanged.

The realisation of this basic concept is the essential task of the film cartoonist. He is obliged to build up his world on a piece of paper in front of him. Whatever results the screen will show, the finished cartoon will be his own creation from beginning to end.

Even after some fifty years of film cartooning, the same

three tools are still the most important: a pencil, a pile of white paper, and ideas. This principle applies in spite of the growth of studios. Departmentalisation has considerably speeded up production, but again technical elaboration has cancelled the time gained by it.

Still, this book is not concerned with the over-elaborate processes developed by the big studios. What we have attempted here is to reveal the basic method of animation, in order to enable you to exploit this medium within your own means as an amateur.

Since the advent of television cartooning has been given its greatest impetus and subsequently new careers have been opened to a great number of young people. I do hope that this simple book will be of use to those who have decided to enter into this new field.

London, June, 1958.

JOHN HALAS.

Contents

	Page
FOREWORD	3
FROM SCRIPT TO SCREEN	9
The Animated Drawing . . .	10
. . . Becomes a Film	11
How to Start	12
MATERIALS FOR ANIMATION	14
The Individual Drawings	14
The Animation Desk	15
The Field of View	17
A Frame Mask	20
Patience and Helpers	21
SPEED AND TIMING	22
Action on the Screen . . .	22
. . . is Timed in Terms of Drawings	23
Rhythm in Timing	24
Timing Shorter Periods	28
Keying the Movement . . .	29
. . . and Breaking It Down	31
Trying It Out	32
BEGINNING TO ANIMATE	34
Natural Movement . . .	34
. . . by Unnatural Drawings	35
Curved Straight Lines . . .	36
. . . and Rounded Squares	38
The Camera Sees It that Way, Too	38
We Can Increase the Illusion	39
Action Along the Speed Railway	40
Size, Distance, Direction	41
Perspective	43
SOME PRINCIPLES OF MOVEMENT	47
How Real Objects Move	47
Movement Causes Distortion	48
Exaggerating Distortion	49

Page

How Much? 50
Making Weight Tell 51
Illusory Elasticity 53
It Doesn't All Move at Once 53
Changing Direction 56
Animated Waves . . . 59
. . . in a Donkey's Tail 61
Secondary Movements 64
Design in Periods 64

CHARACTERS AND SCRIPT 66
Our Actors . . . 66
Take Shape 67
Simple Shapes . . . 68
. . . Become Personalities 73
The Story is Planned . . . 76
. . . in Terms of Action 76
The Story Must Run Smoothly 77
Scenes Must be Linked Up 78
And Now a Complete Script 81

MAKING THINGS EASIER 83
Less Drawing with the Same Effect 83
Making One Picture do the Work of Several 83
Economy in the Background . . . 85
. . . in Perspective . . . 87
. . . and in Scripting 87

PRODUCING THE CARTOON 91
Teamwork Counts 91
The Pictures are Built Up . . . 92
. . . from Initial Keys . . . 93
. . . to the Final Animation 93
Our Means may be Limited 94
Simplifying Matters 98
Half Tones 98
Finishing the Scenes 99
Making a Camera Chart 100
Using Colour 102

PHOTOGRAPHY 103
What the Camera Must Do 103
Further Refinements 104
The Stand for the Camera 105
The Animation Board 106
The Pressure Plate 107
Uniform Lighting 108
The Film to Use 109

Page

Making Tests	112
How to Expose	112
Controlling Exposure	113
Making an Exposure Test	113
Accurate Focusing	115
Fades	116
Mixes	117
Wipes	117
Tracking	118
Double Exposure	119
Just a Few More Aids	120
INDEXED GLOSSARY	121

From Script to Screen

A cartoon film like a painting or photograph, a mouse trap or a motor car, must begin as an idea.

But the modern cartoon film has more in common with the latter pair than the former; it is essentially a manufactured article, and the process of manufacture is continually becoming more and more complicated and specialised. The painter and photographer are able to convert their idea directly into the finished article. Their success or otherwise is determined only by their own creative and technical ability.

The professional producer of cartoon films is much less fortunate. The success of the final result is not determined by his skill alone. His idea must filter through many minds and many pairs of hands, and must be kept alive in the process. If the minds and hands are not able to contribute some part of their own viewpoint and originality, as well as their skill, the idea is likely to die of tedium during the long days of production.

But if there is too much originality, too many viewpoints, the idea will come off the conveyer belt in such an unrecognisable and inferior form that it might just as well have died anyway. The conveyer belt in a cartoon film factory has the disadvantage of being a human, not a mechanical one.

At each of the many stages of such an involved process, something unfortunate can happen to the idea. And very little time is available, if production is continuous, for experimenting in new approaches and techniques.

The amateur working alone or with a small group of friends, should have a greater opportunity to achieve spontaneity and freshness of approach, because his idea will not have to pass through such a tortuous channel before it emerges on to the screen.

The following chapters try to explain to him the fundamentals of successful animation and film making, and to suggest methods of reducing the amount of labour involved, without falling far below professional standards in purely technical matters. The rest is up to him.

The Animated Drawing . . .

Movement on the cinema screen depends on a phenomenon known as *persistence of vision.*

If a series of objects is presented in rapid succession, the eye will momentarily retain the image of each of them after the next has taken its place, so that the interrupted succession appears to be continuous. If the position of each object is, progressively, slightly different, an illusion of movement will result.

In live action cine films this succession of slightly different images is provided by the moving subject itself. Its movement is *analysed* and broken up by the cine camera which automatically photographs slices of that movement in rapid succession 16 times a second in a silent film or 24 times a second in a sound film. The finished film therefore carries a sequence of images, each slightly different from the one before it. In this way 16 (or 24) such images make up a movement or cycle of movement which actually lasts one second.

The projector throws these successive images onto the screen one after another at the same speed at which they were produced on the film. The individual images are *synthesised* again, and the subject appears to move in exactly the same way in which it actually did move in front of the camera.

In a cartoon film, the *animator* takes the place of the live-action camera. His job is to analyse the movement he wishes to portray, and then produce it as a series of drawings. These will eventually appear as a sequence of images on the finished film, 16 or 24 being required for each second of movement.

But merely to copy actual movement is not enough. The camera's analysis is mechanical. The animator's is essentially personal and creative. Apart from artistic ability, the whole secret of the animator's technique is the realisation of how and when actual movement must be exaggerated and distorted in order to produce a pleasing result on the screen.

. . . *Becomes a Film*

Professional studios producing cartoon films in colour and accompanied by sound, have developed a form of organisation dividing the work into specialised departments.

The amateur who decides to embark on a cartoon film of his own will probably use neither sound nor colour, and each department will probably consist of himself with, at most, a team of two or three of his friends. The organisation can be simple or more elaborate.

Nevertheless, his work will progress more smoothly, if he follows professional practice in miniature, simplifying and adapting it to his own needs.

So let us have a look first at professional methods.

The first stage on the journey from idea to film is the illustrated script, which describes the action and also sound and colour in broad terms, verbally and visually.

Then a more detailed script breaks down the whole film into scenes, states the time each action will take, and establishes a rhythm to which the composer sets his music.

The sound track is recorded next and analysed so that the action can be synchronised with it.

The characters and settings are designed, and a *layout* drawing made for each scene.

The animation department can now get to work. From it a torrent of paper will eventually flow, each sheet bearing a drawing of a character in a state of suspended animation.

When all these sheets are photographed on film frame by

frame and viewed in succession in the projector, the drawings will walk and talk, but before then they must go through several more processes.

The paper flood is directed to the tracing department, where each drawing is traced in a fine flowing line on a thin sheet of celluloid (*cell* for short).

Meanwhile the background artists have painted the backgrounds against which the action of each scene takes place.

Colours are chosen for the moving characters and objects to harmonise with the backgrounds and the shapes outlined on the cells are filled in with these colours. Each animation drawing has now become an opaque coloured patch on a transparent sheet.

Now the camera department takes over. The still part of each scene—the background—is fixed firmly under the camera, and the moving part, the cells, are placed over it, building up the complete scene. Each cell is put into position in turn and photographed.

The roll of exposed negative is sent to the processing laboratory, from which positive prints (the *rushes*) are returned.

Each day's rushes are viewed on the screen, exulted or groaned over, and assembled in order (the *cutting copy*).

The cutting copy is matched to the sound track, and eventually a *married print* is received, with the sound and picture on the same film.

For better or for worse, the film is complete.

How to Start

The greatest danger to guard against is loss of enthusiasm. A cartoon film involves a great deal of hard work. So don't start out on a complete film all at once.

Just have a bit of fun trying out odd bits of animation, with very simple "pin" figures, which will develop later into more complicated characters.

When you have sufficient confidence to start on your

Production Number One, make it short and simple. Spend plenty of time preparing the script.

But when the script is finished, stick to it. Don't elaborate it as you go along, or the film may never get finished.

Have one person in charge. Your friends can contribute, but your—the director's—decision must be final!

Complete each scene separately—animation, tracing, painting, background and photography. Seeing Scene 1 on the screen will give you much greater enthusiasm to tackle Scene 2 and make it even better.

Don't amass piles of animation drawings which nobody feels inclined to trace and paint.

And above all, don't weaken! Production Number One will be good, but Production Twenty-One will be a masterpiece.

Materials for Animation

Irrespective whether this is our first attempt at a cartoon, or a million dollar Hollywood production, the only tangible result of all film-making efforts is a strip of celluloid with a lot of little pictures on it. The brilliance of our direction, the magnificence of our settings, or the beauty of our drawings have absolutely no value in themselves, but only in the tiny reproductions as they pass in procession through the gate of the projector.

So, in order to learn something about making cartoon films, let's start where we hope to finish by taking a look at a strip of 16 mm. film.

The Individual Drawings

The film carries a series of rectangular pictures, called *frames.*

They are separated from each other by a narrow margin of unexposed film known as the *frame mask.*

At the corners of each frame there is a *sprocket hole*, by which the film is guided through the projector, and held momentarily in the *gate.*

While it is in the gate, that is, during the time it is being projected on to the screen, the frame of film must be held absolutely still, and must always occupy exactly the same position as the one before and the one following. Otherwise the picture on the screen would jitter, still objects would not remain still, and moving objects would move in a very erratic way. So the function of the sprocket holes is to *register* each frame of film in its correct position.

Each frame must, therefore, occupy exactly the same position on the film relative to its set of sprocket holes. The standard by which the movement of an object may be judged is its position in the frame, relative to the sprocket holes.

To convert our empty strip of film into a cartoon film, we must put a drawing into every frame. It is possible to do this by drawing direct on to the film, and there have been actually several attempts at this technique, both professional and amateur, sometimes with very unusual and interesting results.

But a more practical and convenient method is to make our drawings on separate sheets of paper, and to photograph these drawings on to the film.

The Animation Desk

To do this, we shall need some substitute for the sprocket holes, so that our drawings will be in correct register. We must be sure that an object can be traced in exactly the same position in successive drawings, and that these drawings can be photographed in the same position on successive frames, with the result that the image of the object will appear still on the screen.

The answer to this problem is a very simple device known as the *animation desk*, or *light box*, which is fitted with *register pegs*.

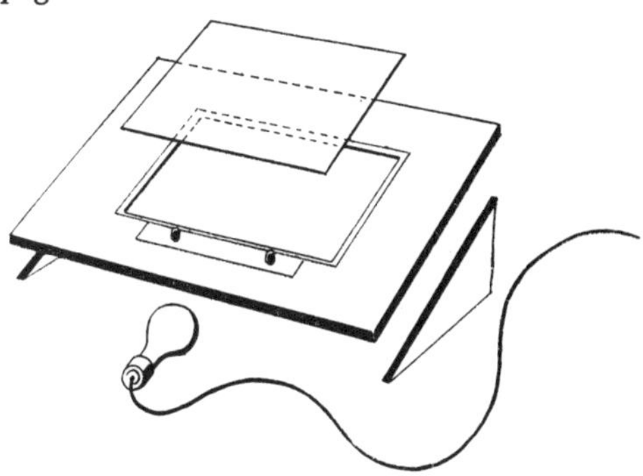

The animation desk, which can be constructed quite

easily, is merely a wooden drawing board, about 15 × 20 ins., tilted at a convenient angle by means of triangular wooden sides.

In the centre of the board is cut a rectangular hole, about the size of the sheets of paper to be used for animation.

Cut a piece of glass to the size of the hole and let it in flush with the surface of the board, supported by strips of beading.

Under this glass panel fit a low-powered electric lamp, so that a number of drawings placed on top of the glass can be seen together when the light is switched on.

Now for the register pegs, probably the simplest, but most important piece of equipment of the cartoonist.

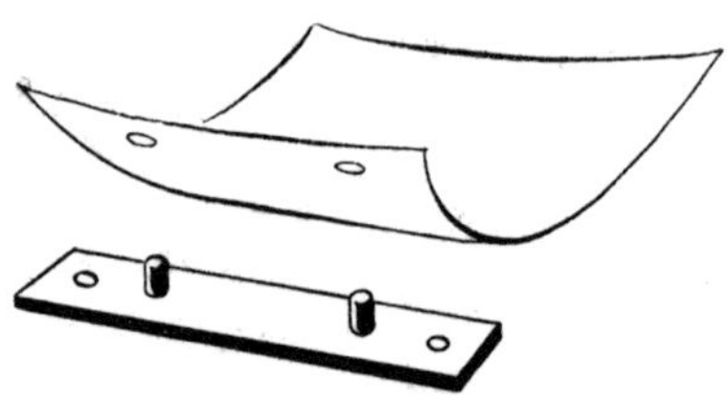

Get hold of a letter punch of the ordinary office filing type. It must be sufficiently rigid so that we can always rely on it to punch two holes of equal diameter with their centres the same distance apart every time.

Punch two holes in a piece of card to act as a template for making the pegs.

These can be metal or wooden dowelling; only they must fit accurately into the punch holes.

When they fit satisfactorily, draw a line with a T-square about one inch below the bottom edge of the glass on the light box, and mark off the centres of the holes equidistant from the centre line of the glass.

Drill the holes and insert the pegs.

They should protrude about $\frac{3}{8}$ inch above the surface of the board and must be absolutely rigid.

As the quality of our animation will depend largely on the accuracy of these pegs, it is worth while taking considerable trouble over fitting them.

An exactly similar set of pegs will be needed on the *camera rostrum* when the drawings are photographed (p. 105).

The Field of View

We must also know the exact size of the drawings to occupy one frame of film. This is the *field* in which the action takes place.

Its position must be fixed in relation to the pegs in the same way as the frame of film is fixed in relation to the sprocket holes.

A frame of 16 mm. film measures about 10.5 × 7.5 mm., while the projection gate aperture is slightly smaller. So if the camera lens is directed on to a surface at right angles to its centre line, it will photograph an area in proportion to these measurements. The drawings must, therefore, always fill an area of these proportions.

The actual size of the area photographed depends on its distance from the lens. A *short focus* (*wide angle*) lens, as shown below right, will take in a larger field than one of *longer focal length*, as shown below left, at the same distance away.

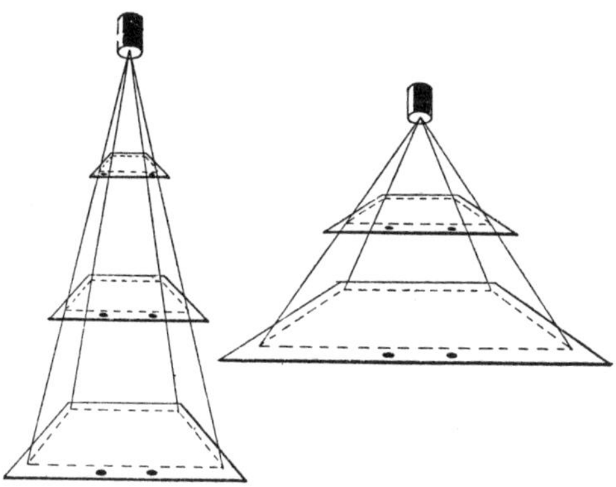

So before we can choose the size of the field for the animation drawings, we must know the focal length of the lens of the camera which will eventually photograph them; and, roughly, the height of the camera above the drawings. This, of course, depends on the space available.

APPROX. 16 mm. CAMERA DISTANCES FOR VARIOUS FIELDS

Standard Field Size (Drawing)	*Camera Distances for Lens of Focal Length* ⅝ *in.* 15–17 *mm.*	1 *in.* 25 *mm.*	1½ *ins.* 37.5 *mm.*	2 *ins.* 50 *mm.*
5 × 3⅝ ins. (12.5 × 9 cm.)	8¼ ins. (20 cm.)	13 ins. (32 cm.)	19½ ins. (47 cm.)	26 ins. (65 cm.)
7 × 5 ins. (17.5 × 12.5 cm.)	11 ins. (27 cm.)	18 ins. (44 cm.)	27 ins. (66 cm.)	36 ins. (89 cm.)
9 × 6½ ins. (22.5 × 16.3 cm.)	14 ins. (34 cm.)	23 ins. (57 cm.)	34 ins. (85 cm.)	45 ins. (110 cm.)
10½ × 7½ ins. (26.3 × 19 cm.)	16 ins. (40 cm.)	26 ins. (65 cm.)	40 ins. (100 cm.)	53 ins. (130 cm.)
12 × 8¾ ins. (30 × 22 cm.)	18½ ins. (46 cm.)	30 ins. (75 cm.)	45 ins. (110 cm.)	60 ins. (150 cm.)

APPROX. 8 mm. CAMERA DISTANCES FOR VARIOUS FIELDS

Standard Field Size (Drawing)	*Camera Distances for Lens of Focal Length* ⅜ *in.* 9 *mm.*	½ *in.* 125 *mm.*	⅝ *in.* 15–17 *mm.*	1 *in.* 25 *mm.*
5 × 3⅝ ins. (12.5 × 9 cm.)	9¼ ins. (24 cm.)	13½ ins. (33 cm.)	17 ins. (42 cm.)	27 ins. (66 cm.)
7 × 5 ins. (17.5 × 12.5 cm.)	14 ins. (34 cm.)	18½ ins. (46 cm.)	23 ins. (57 cm.)	37 ins. (92 cm.)
9 × 6½ ins. (22.5 × 16.3 cm.)	18 ins. (45 cm.)	24 ins. (60 cm.)	30 ins. (75 cm.)	48 ins. (120 cm.)
10½ × 7½ ins. (26.3 × 19 cm.)	21 ins. (52 cm.)	28 ins. (68 cm.)	34 ins. (85 cm.)	56 ins. (135 cm.)
12 × 8¾ ins. (30 × 22 cm.)	24 ins. (60 cm.)	32 ins. (78 cm.)	40 ins. (110 cm.)	64 ins. (155 cm.)

The distances are measured from the camera lens.

APPROXIMATE 9.5 mm. (SILENT) CAMERA DISTANCES

Standard Field Size (Drawing)	*Camera Distances for Lens of Focal Length* $\frac{5}{8}$ *in.* 15–17 *mm.*	20 *mm.*	1 *in.* 25 *mm.*	$1\frac{1}{2}$ *ins.* 37.5 *mm.*	2 *ins.* 50 *mm.*
5 × 4 ins. (12.5 × 10 cm.)	$9\frac{1}{4}$ ins. (24 cm.)	12 ins. (30 cm.)	$15\frac{1}{2}$ ins. (38 cm.)	23 ins. (57 cm.)	30 ins. (75 cm.)
7 × $5\frac{1}{2}$ ins. (17.5 × 14 cm.)	13 ins. (32 cm.)	$16\frac{1}{2}$ ins. (40 cm.)	21 ins. (52 cm.)	31 ins. (76 cm.)	40 ins. (100 cm.)
9 × $7\frac{1}{8}$ ins. (22.5 × 18 cm.)	$16\frac{1}{2}$ ins. (40 cm.)	21 ins. (52 cm.)	27 ins. (66 cm.)	40 ins. (100 cm.)	54 ins. (132 cm.)
$10\frac{1}{2}$ × $8\frac{3}{8}$ ins. (26.3 × 21 cm.)	$19\frac{1}{2}$ ins. (47 cm.)	24 ins. (60 cm.)	31 ins. (75 cm.)	47 ins. (120 cm.)	62 ins. (150 cm.)
12 × $9\frac{1}{2}$ ins. (30 × 24 cm.)	22 ins. (53 cm.)	28 ins. (68 cm.)	35 ins. (85 cm.)	52 ins. (130 cm.)	70 ins. (170 cm.)

The distances are measured from the camera lens.

It is best to standardise on a few set sizes, and adjust camera distance and lens accordingly. This is much better than having to chop and change constantly the scale of the drawings.

The best standard size is 9 × $6\frac{1}{2}$ ins. (22.5 × 16.3 cm.), and our frame mask (p. 20) is designed for that size. We can, however, go down to about 5 × 4 ins., or up to about 12 × 9 ins.

If the drawings are too small, any roughness will show up much more when the film is projected.

Too large drawings, on the other hand, are unwieldy and cause much more work.

We must now get a supply of paper, in sheets large enough to contain this field with a margin all round. It will need to be a large supply; a cartoon studio has a paper consumption rivalling that of any government department!

The cheapest and most easily obtained paper suitable for animation is probably copy typing paper in quarto sheets, measuring $10\frac{1}{4}$ × $8\frac{1}{4}$ ins. (about 25 × 20 cm.). This size will allow for a field of 9 × $6\frac{1}{2}$ ins. (22.5 × 16.3 cm.), which is roughly the screen proportion.

A Frame Mask

Assuming that this size of field fits in with our other requirements, we now make a *frame mask* which is really an enlarged copy of the frame of film on which our drawings will eventually appear.

On a piece of card the same size as a quarto sheet of paper draw a rectangle 9 × 6½ ins. (or 9 × 7½ ins. for 9.5 mm.), leaving a margin of 1½ ins. on one long side.

Punch two register holes centrally at the bottom edge of the wide margin (which will be the bottom of the screen) and cut out the rectangle.

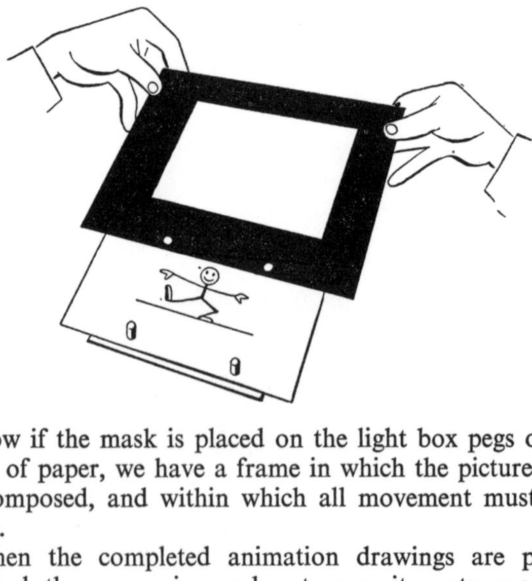

Now if the mask is placed on the light box pegs over a sheet of paper, we have a frame in which the picture must be composed, and within which all movement must take place.

When the completed animation drawings are photographed, the camera is merely set up on its rostrum so that the lens will take in the area within the frame mask. The register pegs are then screwed down on to the baseboard in the same position as the punch holes in the mask. When each drawing in succession is placed on these pegs, and an exposure made, it will occupy exactly the same position on the frame of film as we have drawn it on the desk; it will be in correct register with all the others.

The frame mask is to the film cartoonist what the view finder is to the cameraman. All our ideas are expressed within its boundaries, and no scene could be planned without it. In fact, the frame mask should be regarded as a window through which we can look into the fantastic world of our cartoon actors and actresses.

In planning movement, we must remember that it can happen not only along and across, but towards and away from our eyes; and also that the mask itself can move, as well as the objects within it, in the same way as the lens of the live-action camera can change its point of view in *panning* and *tracking* shots.

This mental habit of thinking of the frame mask as a view finder will help to avoid a flat stereotyped point of view, and bring life, depth and perspective into our scenes.

Patience and Helpers

The only other materials required for animation are pencils, rubbers, and an inexhaustible supply of patience.

The amount of work necessary to make even a short cartoon film, although not quite the "thousands and thousands of drawings" popularly imagined, is quite formidable, especially for one person.

For this reason it is permissible, though perhaps not very polite, to list as "materials" the group of enthusiastic helpers whom the would-be animator should gather around him.

If there is no division of labour, inspiration is likely to lapse rapidly into tedium. Cartoon films are essentially a team job, and forming a team and working with it is half the fun.

Speed and Timing

Very great liberties can be taken with the element of time in a cartoon film. The results can be amusing or instructive. In fact, this is one of the reasons why cartoon films, imaginatively used, can be valuable for teaching. We can speed up the passing of a whole geological era into a few seconds, or watch an electron revolving round its nucleus.

But to begin with our concern is to make animated movements appear as natural and realistic as possible. Careful observation of the time and rhythm of movements is as important as the analysis of the movement itself.

Action on the Screen . . .

The speed of a movement on the screen depends on the number of frames it occupies on the film, and the speed at which the film is projected.

The more frames a movement takes, the longer that shot will take to go through the camera and the projector and the slower it will appear on the screen.

The fewer frames, the faster it will seem.

The speed of projection has been standardised at 16 frames per second for silent films, 24 frames per second for films with a sound track and at 25 frames per second for television. For simplicity's sake we do not consider television in this book as even professionals work to the simplest time unit of 24 frames per second.

We time animation in seconds plus fractions of a second.

Now we can divide 24 frames per second into the following convenient, fractional parts:

1/24 second = 1 frame
1/12 second = 2 frames

1/8	second	=	3 frames
1/6	second	=	4 frames
1/4	second	=	6 frames
1/3	second	=	8 frames
1/2	second	=	12 frames
2/3	second	=	16 frames
3/4	second	=	18 frames
1	second	=	24 frames

The speed of 16 frames per second divides into:

1/16	second	=	1 frame
1/8	second	=	2 frames
1/4	second	=	4 frames
1/2	second	=	8 frames
3/4	second	=	12 frames
1	second	=	16 frames

If we project at 24 frames per second, we have 10 different units for timing movement, whereas at 16 frames we have only 6. Thus sound speed offers a much finer means of expressing the subtleties of a movement.

So, although it means more work in animation, it is better to animate for sound speed of projection, even if our film is a silent film, provided the projector available allows it to project at the higher speed.

In this book *figures given as examples of timing will refer to sound speed* (24 frames per second). To convert them to their equivalent at 16 frames per second, multiply by 2 and divide by 3. As it is impossible to divide single frames into fractions, the nearest whole number will have to serve.

. . . is Timed in Terms of Drawings

Before starting any animation, whether simple or complicated action, we must first decide on its speed. From this we shall know the number of drawings needed.

We must develop a sense of timing, first, to estimate in seconds the total time taken by our sequence of action, and then to split it into fractions of seconds for the more detailed timing of parts of the movement.

So a *stop watch*, or an ordinary watch with a legible second hand should be part of our equipment.

The rest is imagination and visualisation, and there is no short cut.

Suppose we want to animate a figure walking straight across the screen.

How long should he take to move right across, and how big are his steps?

There are no definite answers to questions like this; timing depends on so many different factors. Successful timing is not a matter of set recipes; each new movement is a new problem. And each problem can only be solved by trial and error: animating the action (even if the drawings are only taken to a rough stage); watching the result on the screen, and learning from mistakes.

In this way we develop a sense of timing and begin to get a feeling for the correct number of frames in different circumstances. We can still make mistakes, even, after years of experience, and can still learn from them.

Rhythm in Timing

Let us get back to the little man who is going to walk across the screen.

Is he fat or thin?

Is he in a hurry?

Is he eager or reluctant to reach the other side?

All these considerations of character will affect the timing.

Then, how close is he to the camera? Remember our frame mask is a view finder; close to the camera is big on the screen.

If he is close up, he will go across quicker.

In long shot, slower.

Again, he might be walking in deep snow, or on a dance floor.

All characters should have their own individual style of walking, varying from the pompous and dignified progress of a solid citizen, to the "hop, skip, and jump" of a child. And every individual style of walk should have its own rhythm and timing.

When you have made up your mind about all this, shut your eyes and imagine the whole of the action.

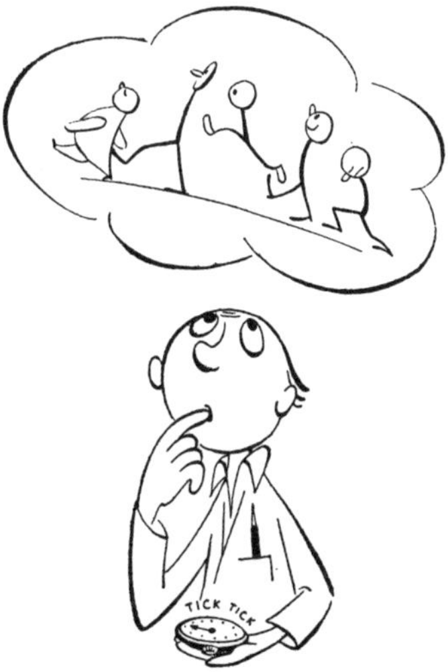

To get it fixed in your mind, it is a good idea to accompany it with a little "dum-de-dum" sort of rhythmic beat.

The little man takes three deliberate steps across a field, and then bumps into a tree.

Like this: "Dum-de-dum-de-dum-de-dum—*bonk!*"

With an eye on the watch, repeat this, say, six times.

Note the total time taken, and divide by six.

This will give a very fair estimate of the time of the whole action.

The time of the separate steps and the *bonk* can then be decided in the same way.

In this case the action is a rhythmic one, and the total time can be divided into four equal parts; one for each step, and one for the bump and fall.

Many actions, of course, break down into less regular divisions than this, and timing them is less simple. But with this method of visualisation we can always find their underlying rhythm, and decide on the timing.

Having picked himself up after the fall, our little man decides to chop down the tree.

He produces an enormous axe, and gets to work.

With a great effort he gets the axe to shoulder level.

Then a pause, and the axe crashes down on the tree.

The momentum of the axe lifts the man off the ground.

After he recovers, he pulls the axe blade out of the tree, and starts the second stroke.

How do we set about timing a movement of this sort?

The first thing to do is to act the movement through for ourselves at the same time chanting, not necessarily aloud, some sort of gibberish to fix the rhythm in our minds.

Remember that the idea is to find a rhythmic division of the movement into equal parts which can be timed by stop watch, and then split up into smaller parts.

The result will probably be something like this: *Up* she goes. *Crash* and down. *Out* and back.

Take the average time for the whole movement in the same way as before. It will probably be 2 seconds, which is 48 frames.

Each of the three sub-divisions will then be 16 frames.

We shall have to know a little more about animation before we can break it down into smaller divisions than this, but a good exercise at this stage would be to visualise a number of movements, and try to time their major divisions.

Try these:

1. Strong man, with large dumb bell. He bends and grips it.

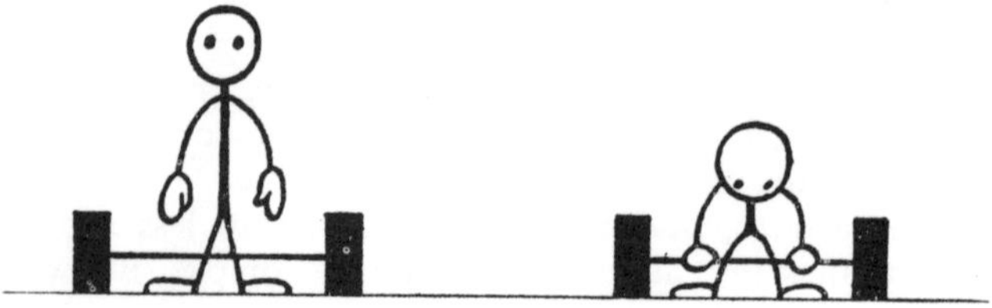

Lifts it in three stages . . . to his waist . . . his chest . . . above his head.

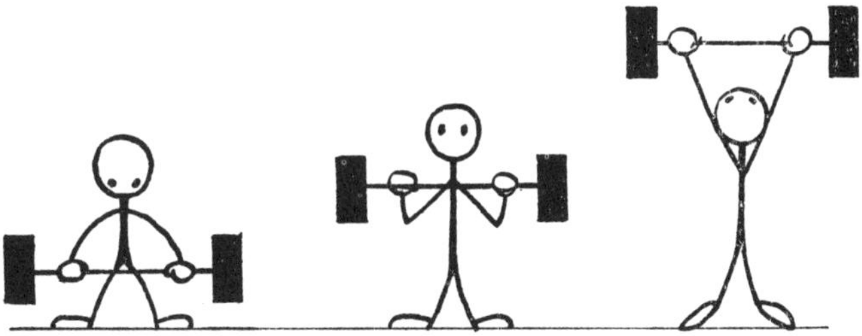

Drops it on his toe. Holding his toe, hops.

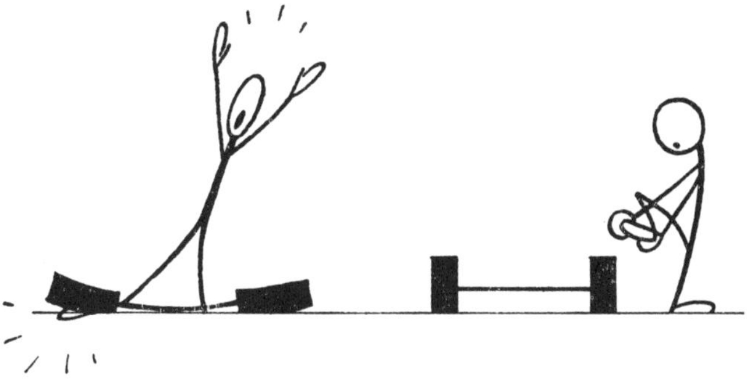

2. Another strong man, swinging the hammer.

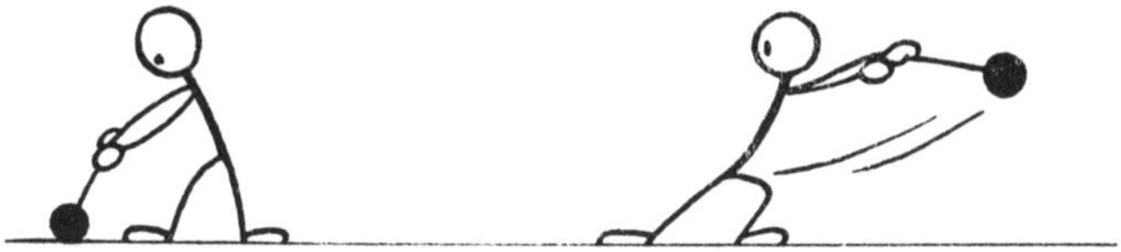

He swings it round six times, getting faster.

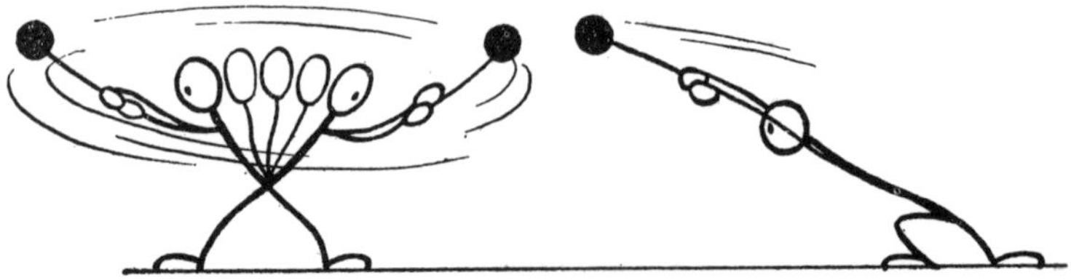

He means to make a record throw, but forgets to let go, and flies off hanging on to the hammer.

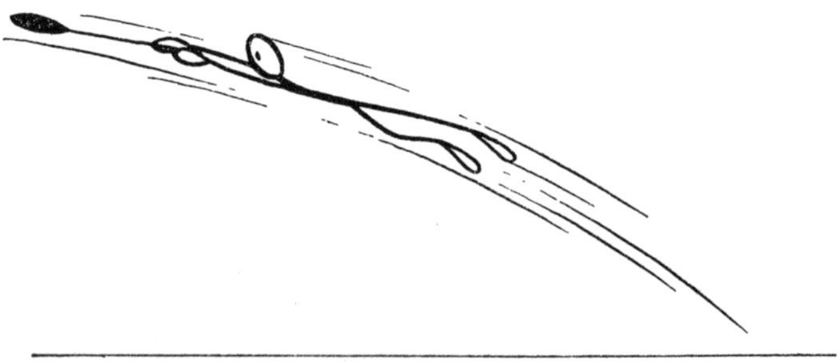

Timing Shorter Periods

When estimating the timing of the finer divisions of a movement, it is useful to be able to divide one second into various fractions, by rhythmic tapping.

First, with the aid of the watch, practise tapping at intervals of one second, the aim being eventually, to be able to tap seconds of reasonable accuracy without referring to the watch.

Then keep one hand tapping seconds, while the other beats 2 beats to the second. This is an interval of 12 frames.

Then double the speed, 4 beats to the second—a 6-frame interval. Double it again, 8 beats to the second—3 frames.

Now change the rhythm and tap 3 beats to the second. This is equivalent to an 8-frame interval. Double—6 beats—4 frames.

Then try 3 beats in 2 seconds, which gives 16 frames.

A motor-driven projector is a valuable aid to timing, as it runs at the standard rate of 16 or 24 frames per second.

If, for instance, on a clear strip of film every 24th frame is black, then on projection at sound speed the screen will be dark for a moment once every second.

Suppose we have decided to animate a walking figure.

The key positions are in this case the two positions with both feet on the ground, at an interval of 12 frames.

Take a strip of clear film, mark off every 12th frame, and paint it black. If it is to be used on a sound projector, continue the black over the sound track area, cut the strip so that its length in frames is a multiple of 12, and join it end to beginning to make a continuous loop. Load this into the projector and switch on.

The black frames on the screen, with the accompanying "clonks" from the speaker will enable you to visualise the movement very clearly, and check the timing.

For irregular movements—one, for instance, where key positions are estimated to occur at frame intervals of 8, 4, 6, 3, and 3, this method is even more valuable.

If you are not satisfied at first, it is easy to make adjustments of a frame or so here and there by scraping off and repainting until you get it right.

Keying the Movement . . .

With the timing decided, there is nothing to prevent us starting work on the animating desk.

First draw in rough form the key positions—the beginning and end of each movement and any position where the movement of any part of the character or object pauses or changes direction. Take again our simple 12-frame walk.

For the sake of clarity, we shall show a man who insists on wearing plus-fours on his left leg and trousers on his right. His right arm is less muscular than his left.

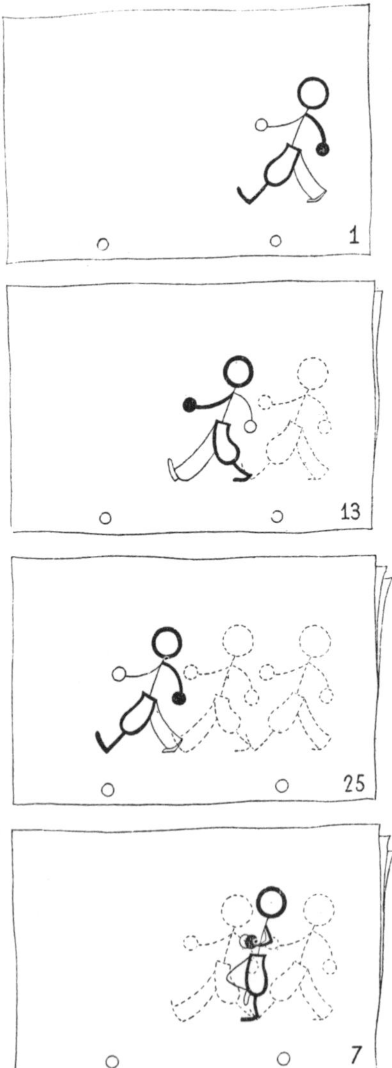

Draw him with both feet on the ground, left foot forward. This is key No. 1. Number it in the right-hand bottom corner.

Then 12 frames after this, his right leg will be on the ground in front of his left leg. Draw this position on another sheet placed over the first, with the light switched on so that drawing No. 1 can be seen. This will be numbered 13.

Then with Nos. 1 and 13 visible beneath it, make No. 25 which will be the same position as No. 1 but moved forward the length of two steps.

And so on until the man has walked across the screen.

. . . *and Breaking It Down*

The next stage is known as the *breakdown*.

Put drawings 1 and 13 on the pegs.

Now draw the middle position between them, which will show the right leg at its highest position moving past the left. This will be No. 7.

The corresponding position between 13 and 25 will be 19, with the left leg off the ground, and so on.

Then comes the in-between stage. Between 1 and 7, make two more drawings 3 and 5, and continue throughout until all the odd numbers are completed, in rough.

This is the stage at which animation should be tested and viewed on the screen.

When movement is so slow that there is only a comparatively small difference between the odd-numbered drawings, a satisfactory result may be got by photographing each drawing twice—using it for two successive frames—instead of once.

This is called *double frame* animation, and obviously saves a considerable amount of work.

Only experience can tell us whether single or double frame is advisable, so a good rule to begin with is to test everything at the double frame stage, and put the additional even-numbered drawings in afterwards, if necessary, when the other rough drawings have been cleaned up.

When shooting the movement at double frame, each drawing should have two numbers: 1—2, 3—4, 5—6, and so on, to avoid confusion.

Trying It Out

Even the most experienced professional animator cannot be sure that his animation will be satisfactory before he sees it on the screen.

In professional studios a large amount of film is used up experimentally to photograph animation drawings just to see whether animation is as good as possible before it passes to the next stage, tracing on to celluloid sheets, and colouring.

Unfortunately, this careful testing, although particularly necessary when learning to animate, is probably too expensive an item in film and processing costs for the amateur. So some method of viewing drawings in rapid succession without having actually to photograph them on film, would be a valuable addition to our list of requirements.

This is a simple gadget on the lines of the "What the Butler Saw" machines which were once a feature of most seaside piers.

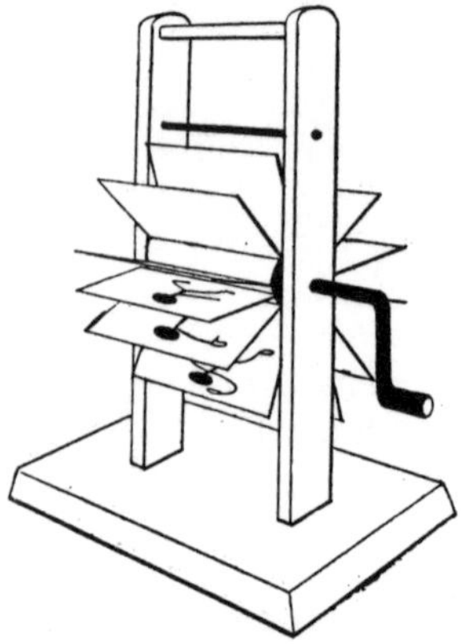

The drawings for 1 second of animation which for this purpose should be made on paper stouter than the usual animation paper, are mounted on a spindle.

This is rotated by a handle, so that each drawing in turn comes up against a stop, and is held stationary for a fraction of a second.

If a series of odd-numbered drawings are mounted in this way, and the handle rotated at a constant speed of 1 turn per second, we have a sufficiently accurate test for timing, single or double frame, and general smoothness of animation.

A little time and ingenuity spent on making this, will save a lot of film.

Beginning to Animate

We have seen that movement on the cine screen is an illusion produced by the rapid succession of slightly different images passing through the projector. Further, if these images are drawings differing from one another in a way similar to the images produced by filming real action with the cine camera, the drawings will seem to come to life because of the persistence of vision of our eyes.

Natural Movement . . .

But even with the live action camera there are limits to what our eyes will accept as continuous movement.

If the camera swings rapidly across a landscape with a prominent vertical feature such as a telegraph pole in the foreground, the pole on the screen will appear to jitter quite a bit as it passes across. The gap between each of the successive images of that pole may have proved too large for our eyes to be able to bridge it with the illusion of its movement.

Jitter of this sort on the screen, which is not caused by a fault in animation, or in the camera, is referred to as *optical jitter*. The type of movement which causes it is known as *unsympathetic* movement.

These unsympathetic types of movement are, however, comparatively rare in live action films, for a number of reasons. The moving objects have as a rule substance and are three-dimensional. They are familiar and easily recognised. The movement takes place against a background which recedes naturally into the distance, and may be also assisted by various kinds of secondary movement, such as the folds and creases in the clothing of the moving person would produce.

In making cartoon films, we have none of these advantages. We have to persuade the eyes and brains of our audience to accept movement which has never actually taken place, of an object which has never actually existed in a space that is merely imagined.

So a technique of animation must be used which ensures that all movements are as sympathetic as possible—as co-operative as possible in creating the necessary illusion.

. . . *by Unnatural Drawings*

This is achieved by a deliberate and carefully considered distortion of the moving forms.

If each frame of a moving figure in a live action film were carefully traced, and the drawings photographed to make a cartoon film, the movement would probably appear very stiff, artificial and jerky.

On the other hand, if each frame of the movement of an animated figure, which appears pleasantly smooth and natural on the screen, is examined individually, the drawings of the figure often appear extremely unnatural.

Let's take our upright pole as a simple example to start with. It has to be animated from

here | to here. |

If the movement is so slow that we can put in a large number of in-betweens

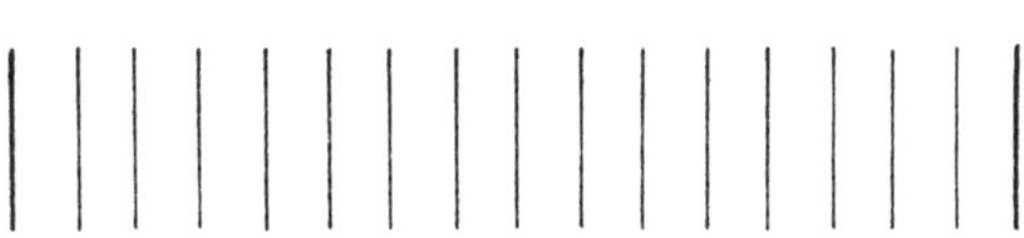

the result will probably be fairly satisfactory; but if we need to speed it up

the movement becomes unsympathetic, as the eye will have difficulty in connecting the separate images.

If the pole now falls over and becomes a horizontal line

——— to be moved to here ———

it can be seen that an even faster movement

will give a smooth and pleasant effect.

Curved Straight Lines . . .

Obviously it is impossible to ensure that all objects will move only along, and never across, their own length.

But very often we can modify the drawings of an unsympathetic movement. We can change the form of the moving object to increase the sympathy of the movement.

Our pole can be bent (distorted) like this, for instance:

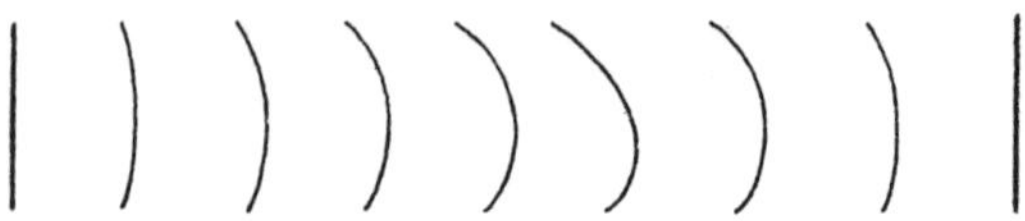

and back the other way:

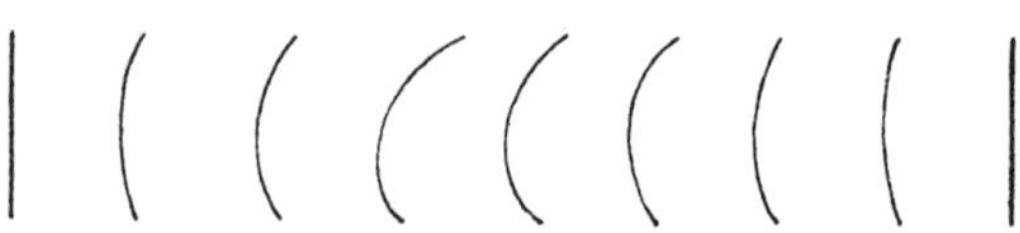

so that we have a sympathetic movement *along* to offset the unsympathetic one *across*.

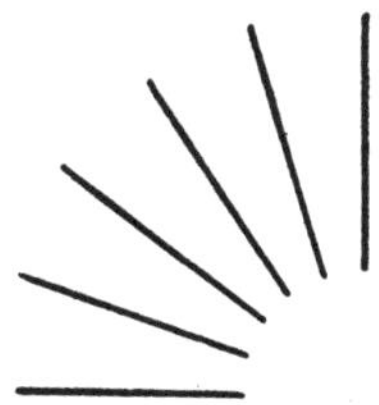

If it is to be raised from horizontal to vertical distortion like this will help going up, and going down.

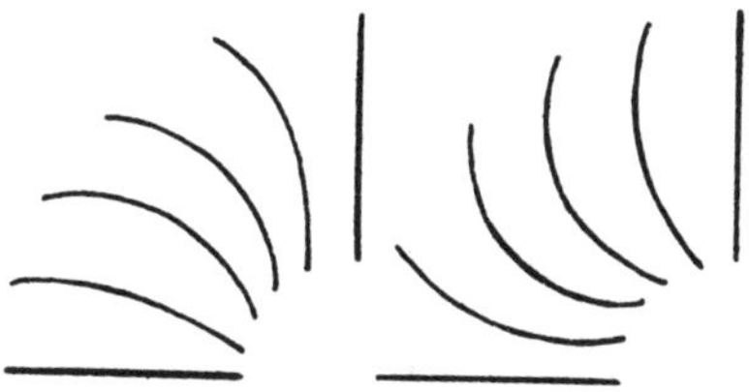

If our pole is now taken as one arm of a little man, and his hand is added to the end of it:

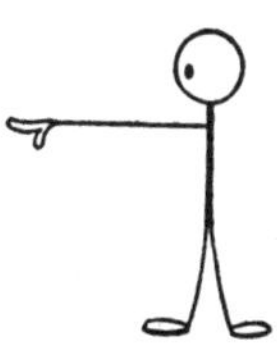

we have a very simple application of this theory to figure animation.

Try some more on the animation desk.

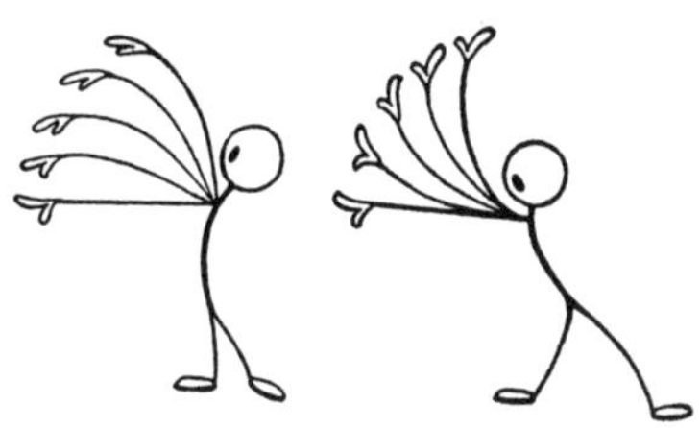

. . . *and Rounded Squares*

Not only lines, of course, but all kinds of solid forms should be distorted in this way, when necessary, to make their movement sympathetic to the eye.

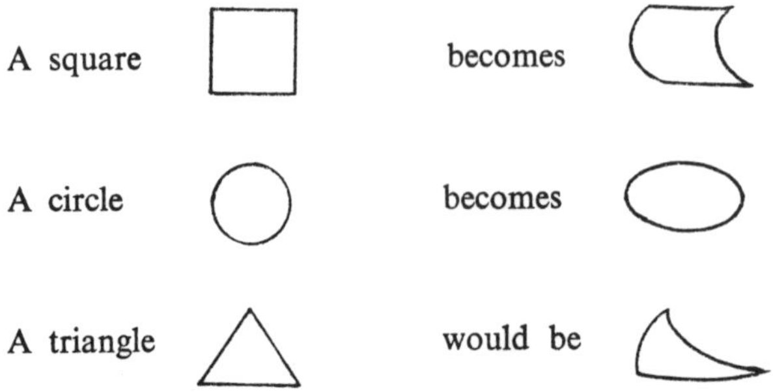

As the speed of the moving shape increases, the necessity for distortion increases too, as the eye has to bridge larger and larger gaps between each drawing.

It is, therefore, advisable to make the shape grow in the direction of its movement as it accelerates.

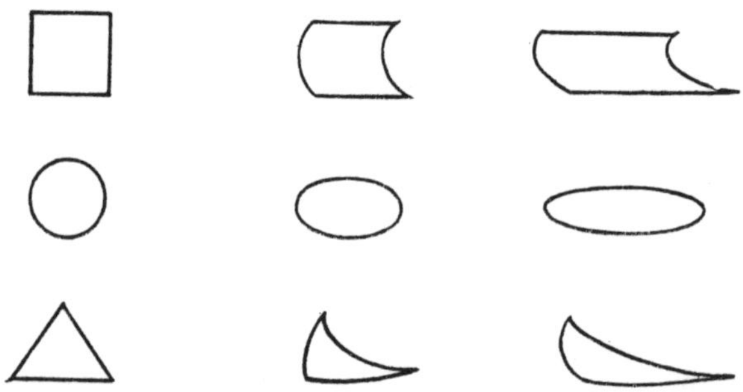

The Camera Sees It that Way, Too

The need for this particular distortion is confirmed by another limitation which the live action camera shows up.

The actual time during which one frame of film is held still in the camera gate while being exposed is about 1/50 second.

If an object is moving too fast for its image to be arrested by this comparatively long exposure, it will show a blurred double image on the side away from the direction of movement.

The extent of this blur will increase as the movement becomes faster, and decrease as it slows down.

Close examination of individual frames show that with a very fast moving object the extent of the blur causes an apparent distortion to the shape of the object which is of exactly the same kind as is introduced into cartoon forms to increase the sympathy of movement.

We Can Increase the Illusion

The blur is obviously of great help in persuading our eyes to accept the illusion of movement. For this reason it is introduced into fast moving forms as a shading of fine lines, called *speed lines* or *swish lines* which continue the form of the object on the side away from its movement.

Theoretically, of course, the lines should not extend further than the outline of the object in the previous drawing. But to get an impressive effect of speed, they are often carried to an exaggerated length.

In some cases the object itself may be omitted, and only the speed lines animated.

As the speed of an object increases, then, the distortion of its form in the direction of movement will increase until speed lines appear.

Then the length of the speed lines increases, until the form of the object gets so blurred that it disappears altogether, and only the speed lines are visible.

As the speed decreases, first the outline of the object appears again. Then the speed lines shorten, then they disappear, leaving the object only slightly distorted, until it stops, and regains its normal form.

Although this theory, like every other theory of animation, has its exceptions, by its intelligent use the comparative speed of the tortoise and the hare, or the Wright plane and a jet aircraft can be very vividly shown.

Action Along the Speed Railway

We can put this theory into practice on the animation desk very simply by taking two points, as far apart as possible within the field, and animating a circle (or some other shape) from the one to the other.

We can take a straight or a curved course at uniform or varying speed, but, for the purpose of the exercise, always in a time of 1 second for the whole movement.

First we must make what is known as a *speed railway*, which is simply the line of the course the circle is to take divided into the number of frames the movement occupies.

Here are a few examples:

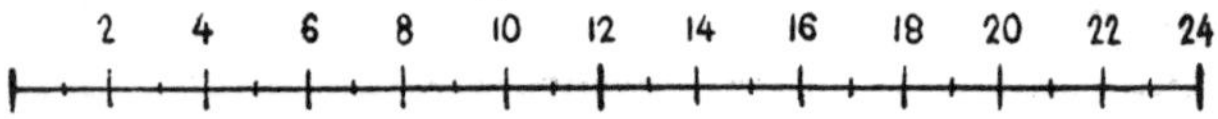

Even speed.

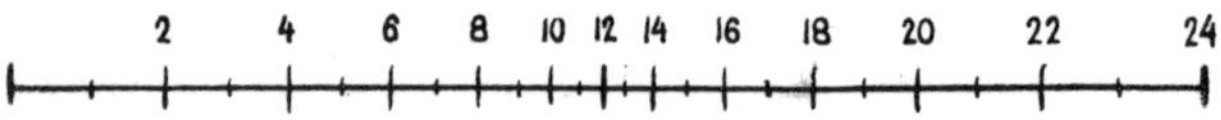

Fast— slow down— speed up.

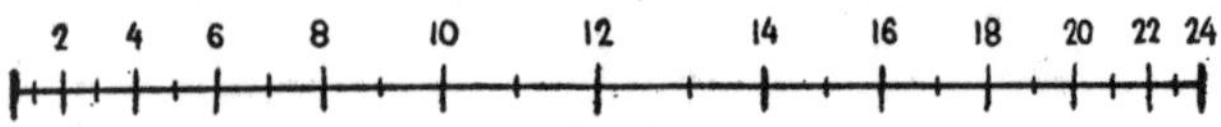

Slow— fast— slow.

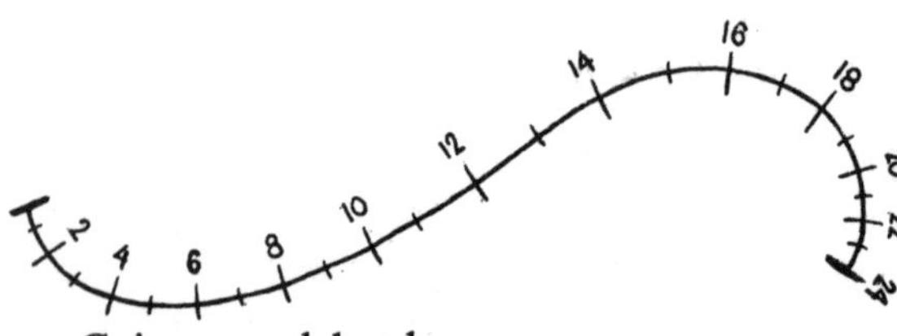

Going round bends.

. . . showing different ways of speeding up and slowing down on straight and curved paths.

These speed railways are the mechanical guides to all animation, not only for the movements of objects, such as our circle, but also to plot the movement of different parts of characters, such as hands, feet, head, etc., so that some parts can be made to move at different speeds to and in different directions from others without confusion when the in-between drawings are put in.

Each point on the line, of course, shows the position of a certain object, according to its number.

It is worth while taking some trouble to practise the division of lines into the correct proportions for various rates of getting faster, and for varying lengths of time of movement.

For even speeds it is easy to calculate the spaces by simple division. But when the speed varies, it is largely a matter of trial and error.

Now when we have prepared our speed railway, we animate the circle along it by using each point as the centre of one drawing. Here we shall have to estimate the amount of distortion required which will be governed by the speed of the circle at any given point.

Size, Distance, Direction

Note that its speed, as distinct from its slowing down or accelerating, will depend on its size. Apparent speed, or the speed seen on the screen, is not the same as actual speed. An aeroplane, looking very small at a height of ten thousand feet, seems to move much slower than one at roof-top height, although the actual speed of both may be the same.

If two objects of the same size, and moving at the same speed, are at different distances from the camera, the nearer one will cross the screen in less time, but the proportion of their own length which they advance for every frame will be the same.

Conversely, if two objects of different sizes are moving at the same speed, the proportion of their own length advanced for every frame will be different.

Here are two circles which are to move through the same distance, from A to B, in the same number of drawings.

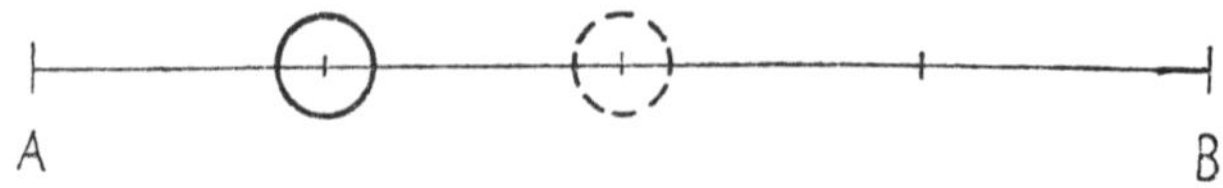

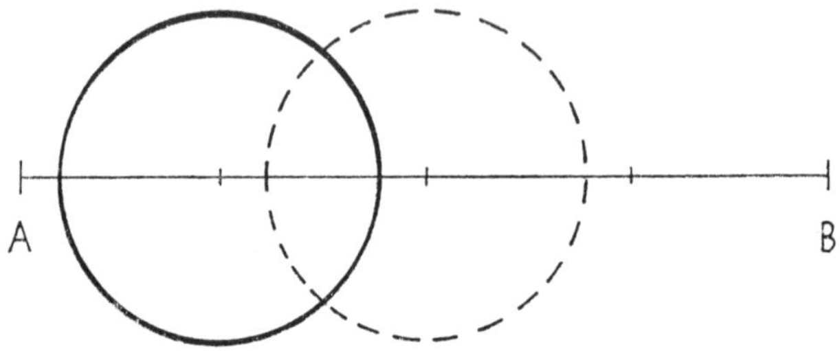

Note the distance in proportion to its own diameter that each circle moves in one frame. Obviously, the small one will be moving much faster than the larger one. It is this factor, the size of the object in relation to the space traversed per drawing that decides the amount of distortion.

The small circle would at this speed require speed lines and the maximum distortion, but the large one needs hardly any distortion at all.

If, instead of the simple circle, we use any kind of moving object, the same principle applies. A motor-car travelling across screen in the foreground, then re-entering the screen on a road in the middle distance, must move the same proportion of its length per frame in both sizes if it is to appear to maintain the same speed.

If the car is followed by a smaller object travelling at the same speed, the smaller object will probably need distortion and speedlines, as its apparent speed—length compared to distance moved—is greater.

Remember, too, that to animate smoothly, an object must assume the line of the course it is following.

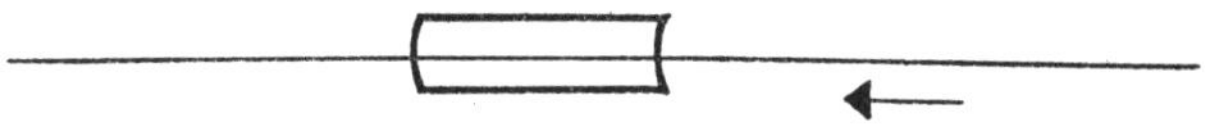

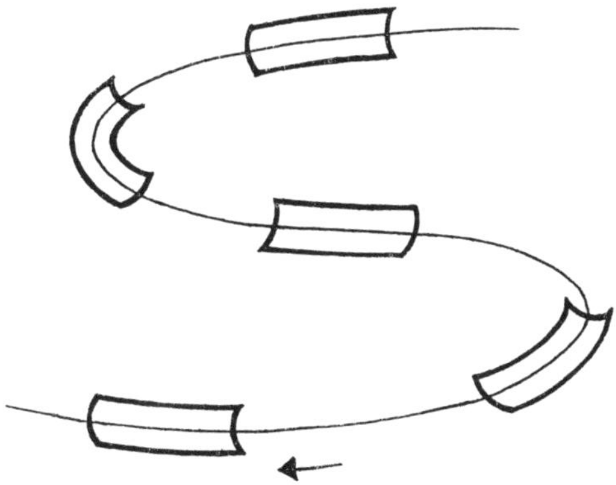

A rectangle, moving along a straight line, remains a rectangle.

But if it moves along a curved line, its sides should be curved—provided it is moving at a sufficient speed to be distorted at all.

Perspective

Assuming that we have passed the previous test to our own satisfaction, in the light of what is shown by the projector, the next step is to animate a simple object in perspective.

The object can be made either to approach or to go away from the camera; increasing or decreasing in size on the screen.

In all perspective animation, it is advisable to lay the thing out properly, complete with T-square, set square, and the rest of the ghastly collection.

The whole effect will be spoiled if the perspective is not accurate. Our eyes can seldom be trusted to judge the perspective of a whole series of drawings as they sometimes can with a single one.

Larger sheets of paper than normal will be needed for this.

Perspective drawing is a conventional way of representing a solid, three-dimensioned object on a flat two-dimensional sheet of paper. It is based on the observation that two parallel straight lines, if placed in any position other than horizontally across the observer's field of view, will appear to converge. If continued, they will meet at a point—the *vanishing point*—on a horizontal line level with the observer's eye—the *horizon.*

The horizon is normally taken to be a little below the centre line of the field of view—in our case the frame mask. If it is lower, the observer or camera, will seem to be looking upwards, if it is higher, downwards.

For dramatic effects, when an object or figure is made to rush "out of the screen", take a low horizon.

A high horizon is useful for a peaceful "toy-town" effect.

To start with, let's take a cube which has to be animated towards the camera, at even speed, and along a straight course. Establish horizon, vanishing points, etc., and draw it in its first position, not too small in screen. Indicate its final position.

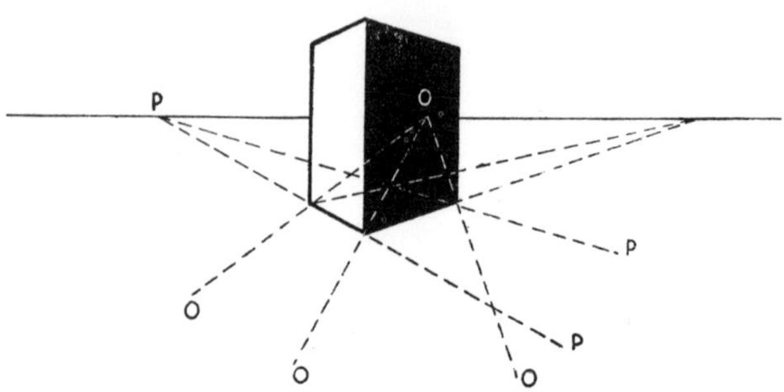

It can advance along the lines of either of its own sides from the vanishing point (lines *P*). Alternatively it can advance along any lines connecting a point on the horizon with its bottom corners (lines *O*).

To reduce the number of lines in the diagrams, we will make it travel along the lines *P*, but the method is the same in either case.

Assuming we want it to move during 1 second, all we need is a series of key points, 1 to 25 along one of these lines. These key points divide the distance the cube travels into equal parts. These parts will, of course, not actually be equal. We are never as fortunate as that.

The cube can then be constructed on each of these points, except for the length of the horizontal sides.

Here some book on perspective comes in useful to tell us how to obtain the lengths of these sides by *measuring points*, but it is usually possible to estimate this quite accurately enough by comparing their lengths with the lengths of the divisions in the line of the course of movement.

When we have drawn the keys, we can get in the in-between drawings by estimation.

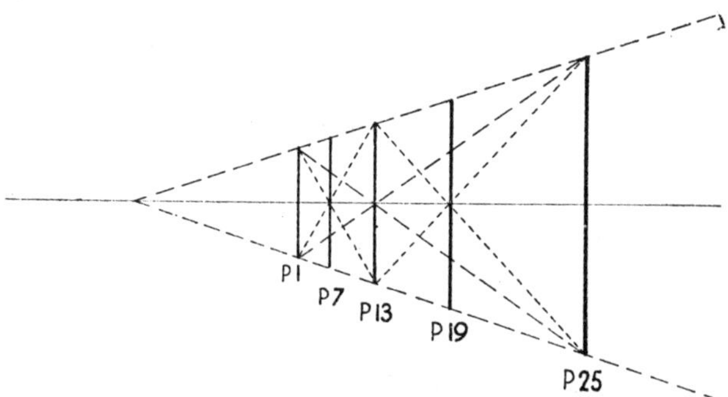

First, connect the top right corner with the vanishing point from which it is to move and extend this line to the right.

Draw a vertical to it from *P*. 25, the final position.

Draw the diagonals of this rectangle.

Drop a vertical from the intersection of these diagonals. It cuts the bottom line at the middle point (*P*. 13) of the cube's journey.

P. 7 and 19 can now be found by more diagonals, and so on. Bob, we hope, is now our uncle!

When the result of this exercise is projected and compared with the last, the value of perspective in adding to the dramatic interest of animation should be very apparent. It presents some fascinating problems to be overcome, as we shall find when we go on to work out some variations on the simple example given.

Try these for a start:

1. Advance the cube on the line *O*.
2. Lower the horizon.
3. Change the vanishing points, turning the cube to a different angle.
4. Lift the cube off the ground as it moves forward, until its underside is visible.
5. Advance on a curved course (Ouch!). The key points for this are best obtained by estimation, using the experience gained in the previous examples. Projecting them is a very complicated matter. But don't forget that the vanishing points will move along the horizon as the cube turns, in following along the curve. Best of luck!

If a figure is being animated to move in perspective—for instance, a man walking up to or away from the camera—the length of his steps must be plotted out in perspective in the same way as the equal stages by which we moved our cube forward. Otherwise the effect will be completely spoilt. Unless the steps in the distance are at least approximately the same length in proportion *to his size* as those in the foreground, he will be likely to hurtle away at jet-propelled speed wearing seven-league boots.

Sometimes this may be funny, but it is more likely to raise a laugh of the wrong sort.

Some Principles of Movement

We should now have reached the stage where we are likely to want to stop playing about with simple shapes, and start making them look like something.

A very brief study of the laws which govern the movement of objects in real life will show us that the distortion which we introduce into the shapes we are animating is not just arbitrary, but has its foundation in nature. The use of distortion, therefore, is the only way which enables us to reproduce movement so that our characters and objects will appear to have weight and solidity, and give a convincing illusion of reality, however fantastically they may behave.

We have so far considered distortion only as an aid to the eyes of our audience in accepting and following movement on the cartoon screen, but it is a most important part of the movement itself.

How Real Objects Move

There are three principles which have a great bearing on the animator's work—the *Laws of Motion* established by Newton.

Their effects will have to be applied to every movement we animate. If we don't apply them, our animation can never be vigorous and natural, and our objects and characters can never look real and solid.

Firstly a body which is still, tends to remain still. In the same way a body which is in motion, tends to remain in motion.

Secondly, the states of stillness and movement of a body can only be changed by the action of an outside force. The body will move in the direct line in which the force is applied, until another force acts to change its direction.

Thirdly, every action causes an equal reaction in the opposite direction.

The animator's application of these rules will probably be a caricature of their application in physical science. But in order to make fun of something, we must have at least a superficial knowledge of it.

The most important of these laws, as far as we are concerned, is the first.

To avoid confusion in the following examples in referring separately to the tendency to remain still, we will call it *inertia*, and a little unscientifically, call the tendency to continue moving *momentum*.

These two control all animation, they are the natural law behind the fantastically unnatural behaviour of cartoon characters which is their chief appeal.

Cartoon people may defy other natural laws, such as gravity, for which they often have complete contempt; but they must always obey the laws of inertia and momentum.

Movement Causes Distortion

Unfortunately, the effects of inertia, in that it actually causes a change in the shape of a body, take place so quickly that they are invisible to the eye, and even to the cine camera. But the high speed camera, taking exposures as brief as 1/10,000 second or even less, can easily record these tiny movements, and it has given us some fine examples on which we can base our observations.

For instance, a golf ball, after it has been struck by the club, but before it starts on its flight, is squashed almost to a flat disc. This is because (like many people we could name) it doesn't want to start moving. The part that *has* to move, because the club is pushing it, crowds forward on to the part which hasn't yet been affected by the force. Then, when its inertia has been overcome, the elasticity of the ball draws it forward into its original shape, and it springs away from the club with tremendous vitality.

In the same way a boot kicking a football sinks right into the ball, which is distorted almost into the shape of a sausage before it springs away.

The reverse effect is illustrated by a ball in flight on its being returned by a stroke from a tennis racket. This time the ball doesn't want to stop, and the part that is still moving pushes forward on to the part which is being forced to stop. Again the ball is squashed flat. It has not sufficient energy to overcome the momentum of the racket, which is moving in the opposite direction and doesn't want to stop either. Although this makes the strings of the racket bulge backwards until they begin to look like a fishing-net, they succeed in bringing the ball to rest. At last the elasticity of the strings and the forward movement of the racket push the ball forward again, its inertia is again overcome, and it zings away.

It is this vitality, this "zing" that we want to get in our animation, and obviously the use of the effects of inertia, wherever possible, will help us.

Exaggerating Distortion

Our problem is time.

The effects we have seen photographed, occurred in a minute fraction of a second. Our smallest unit of time is 1/16 or 1/24 second, so if we make the squash happen on only one frame, its duration will be enormously exaggerated. Happily this, for some reason, doesn't seem to matter, provided the distortion is exaggerated in space as well as time.

In really dynamic movement, we have to carry distortion to the utmost.

The football must, for one frame, be a sausage.

For one frame the tennis racket must be a fishing-net.

This may sound very daring, but, it does actually work, and strangely enough will look very much more real than if we don't risk such exaggeration.

This distortion is known to the animator as *squash*, and is used in varying degrees in all movement, fast or slow.

It is the means by which cartoon movement, a thing in itself false and unnatural, can be made to look realistic on the screen.

For this reason, cartoon characters are designed to be pulled and pushed into all sorts of shapes and still remain recognizable.

Apart from the use of squash to make movements natural and convincing, the exaggeration of the effects of inertia is often the basis for a cartoon story and is the main source from which many films derive their humour. In that case, distortion is made very obvious and becomes a movement in itself, instead of merely part of a movement.

However, the animator should concentrate first on achieving natural-seeming movement before attempting animation of this type.

How Much?

The degree of squash and the number of drawings on which the squash is animated depends on three characteristics of the objects themselves:

First, the *speed* at which they are moving when they come into contact with the force that stops them; or the *power of the force* which starts them.

Second, the *weight* (or, to be exact, the *mass*) of the objects.

Third, the *material* of the objects, particularly the *elasticity* of this material.

These three factors, however, will sometimes contradict each other, as we shall see.

When this happens, we can only make up our minds which is the most important, and act accordingly. Then, when we find we have chosen the wrong one, start again.

The word "squash" is engraved on every animator's heart, and wherever animation is being discussed and criticised, "too much squash" or "not enough squash" is a constant cry.

Let's consider the three in turn.

The first is the simplest. Obviously a ball will squash less on bouncing if it is travelling slowly.

A body falling from six feet, will squash less than one falling from sixty feet (especially if it's a human body!).

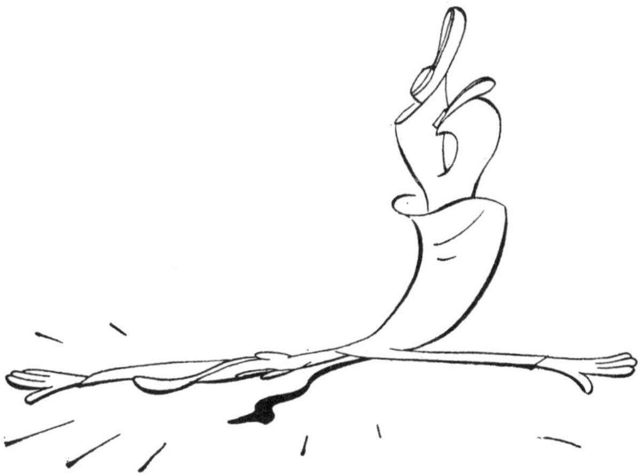

A slow lob is much less punishing to a tennis ball than a smashing drive.

But this factor has little effect on the speed of squash. That is more dependent on the weight.

Making Weight Tell

This is where contradictions begin to occur.

As a general rule, a heavy object will squash more; and more slowly than a lighter one.

Consider the elephant, an animal whose loose flesh and skin, rather floppy feet and flapping ears make him visibly squash when walking, in a most cartoony way. He certainly looks his weight.

Compare him with the giraffe, also a large and heavy animal, but one whose taut and rigid structure does not visibly alter when he walks. This gives him a deceptive appearance of lightness.

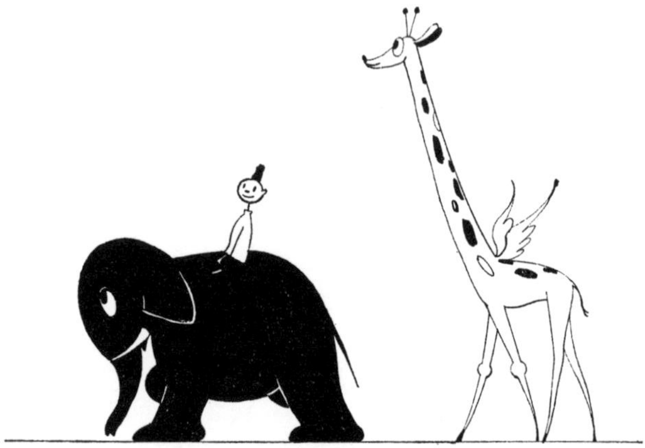

So, to obtain an effect of lightness, squash should not be much exaggerated, and should occupy only one or two frames.

For great weight, very much exaggerated squash, happening comparatively slowly; five, six, or even more frames could be used.

But now imagine a large soap bubble, floating very slowly to earth. As it touches, it could be shown to squash slowly down to an oval shape, and then contract back again with a slight, slow bounce, and repeat the process till it comes to rest, behaving much as our general rule tells us, an iron weight should be animated.

Here, of course, the speed of descent is one thing which accounts for the anomaly, and another is elasticity. The bubble's light weight is expressed by its tenuous outline and iridescent colour, and its elasticity is the important factor to be expressed by movement.

Illusory Elasticity

In animation, all substances are endowed with elasticity they do not possess, because we always have to exaggerate distortion.

Lumps of iron, or concrete, in cartoon motion, can only be given the apparent weight of concrete and iron, if they behave in a way in which these conservative and inelastic materials would never dream of behaving in real life.

But if everything must bend and stretch as if it were made of rubber, then something that is actually made of rubber must bend and stretch to an infinitely greater extent, and take much more time over it.

So, if the quality to be emphasised in an object in movement is its elasticity, give it very much more, and slower and therefore more visible) distortion.

The only factor which limits the time taken by squash in all these cases is that it must not be visible for long enough to be confused with the normal shape. If we are conscious of the distortion as a thing in itself, and not as a part of the whole movement, it is too slow.

And, of course, when an object comes to rest after violent movement and is to be held stationary for any length of time, it must be seen in its undistorted form.

However much the distortion, the total volume of the squashed object must appear to remain more or less the same.

It Doesn't All Move at Once

In making any object start or stop moving, then, even if it is not such fast movement as the examples we have considered, we have to remember that a part of it will start moving before the rest has started, and stop before the rest has stopped.

The force, or impetus, is transferred through the substance of the object, and effects each part in turn.

Each part is reluctant to move or come to rest before it must.

The part that moves or ceases to move first is the part to which the force is directly applied.

A great deal of quiet fun can be got out of these effects. For instance, here is a pin man pushing a heavy truck.

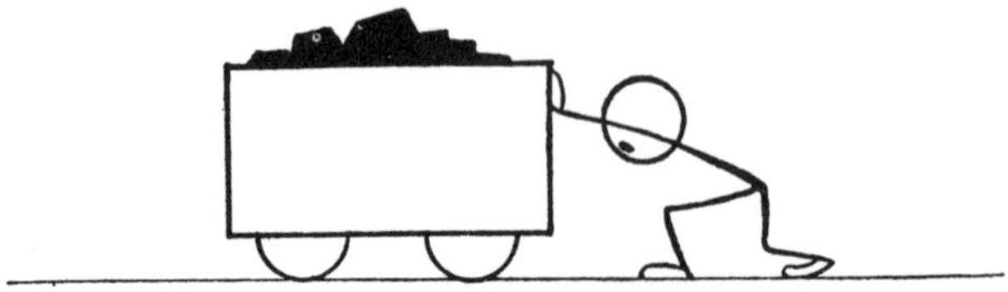

The part that must move is the part he is pushing.

It is heavy, so it will start to move slowly. The rest doesn't want to move.

So, the first result (with his feet moving rapidly and slipping back, to express the magnitude of his efforts) is only to distort the truck like this:

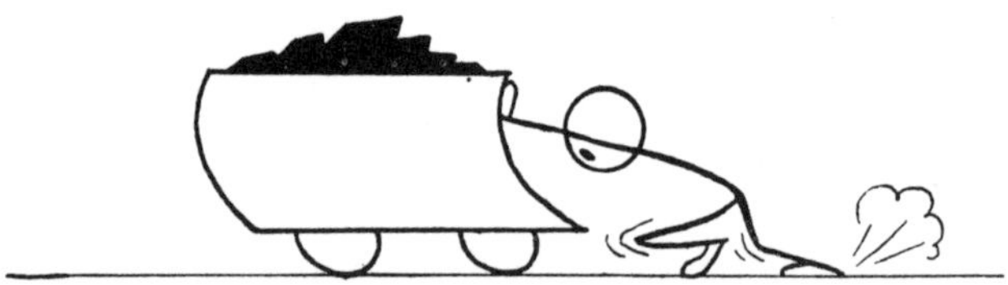

Then he overcomes the inertia.

The shape of the truck returns to normal, and the movement continues.

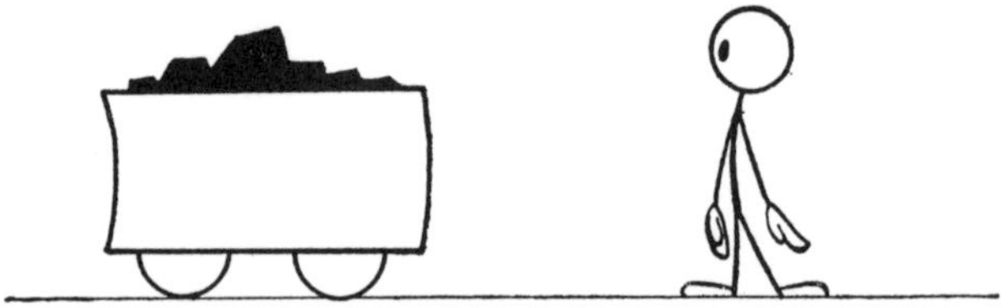

To stop the truck, another force must be brought to bear; either friction or an obstruction.

If it is going to be friction, the man stops pushing, and the truck continues.

Friction acts first on the wheels, so they slow down, and finally stop.

As they slow down, the rest of the truck still has momentum and wants to go on. So again it is slightly distorted before it comes to rest.

With an obstruction the distortion will be greater, as the stop is more sudden.

The momentum of the truck tends to wrap it round the buffers, in the same way as cars tend to wrap themselves round lamp posts.

The greater the speed, the greater the "wrap".

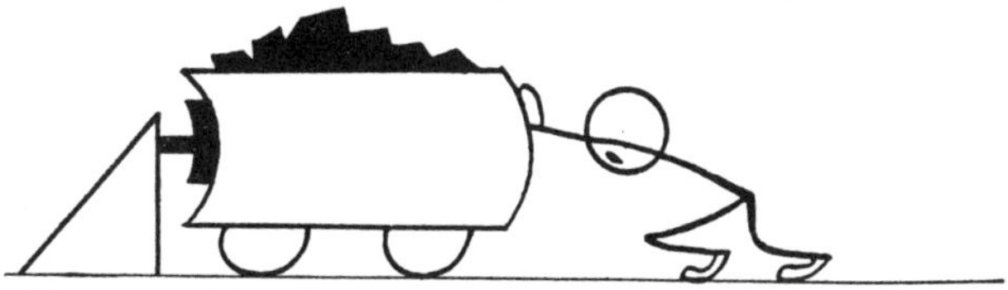

The man, if he is fool enough to go on pushing, will be the next object to squash while the truck is returning to normal.

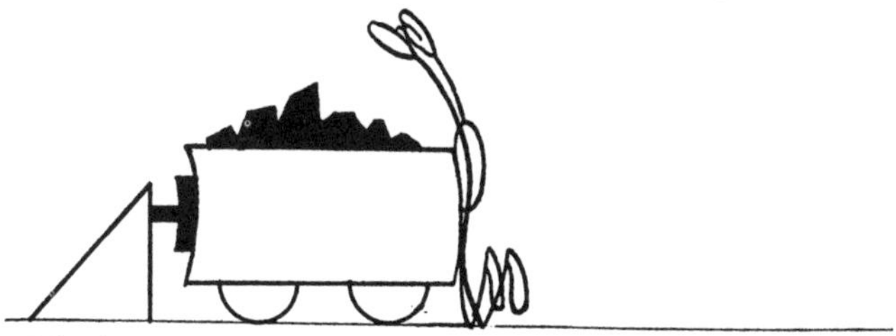

The last object to return to normal is the man.

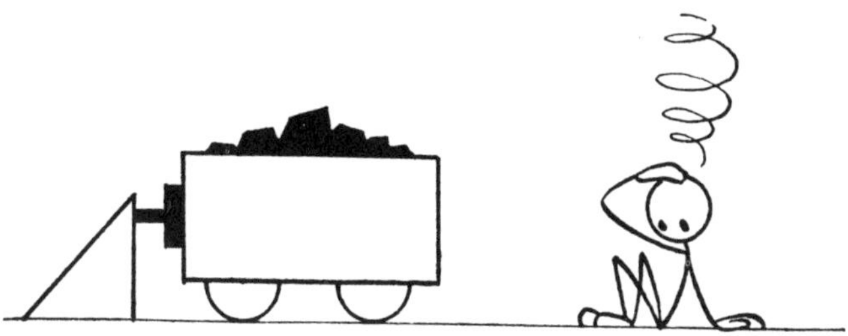

This passing on of the squash from one object or figure to another, or from one part of an object to another, is known as a *concertina movement*, and has many applications. Invent some more.

Make sure, however, that the squash does not happen before the object meets the force that causes it. There must always be one drawing showing the object un-distorted in contact with whatever is going to cause it to distort.

Here are a few more simple examples. Try thinking up a gag which arises directly out of the movement, to enliven them.

1. A ball bouncing on a hard surface. This and the following ones will be what is known as a "repeat movement", as the first key—the ball at its maximum height above ground—will also be the last, and will start the movement over again. The same drawings can be repeated an indefinite number of times. Suggested timing, 16 frames for each complete movement.
2. A pin man hitting the side of a post with a large stick. The point here is that after the stick touches the post, momentum will still carry its end forward, and the stick will bend round the post, before it returns.
3. Same pin man hitting the top of the post with a heavy mallet. Both the mallet and the post will squash.

Changing Direction

When a moving object changes direction, the second rule of motion comes into play—an object moves in the direction of the force that starts it, and only another force, in another direction, can make it alter its course.

The direction from which the impetus comes is a very important factor in the shape and behaviour of animated forms.

This can best be illustrated by taking as an example the

animation of a stick with another stick hinged to it at one end, which is free to move from side to side. The whole thing is moved by a hand grasping the lower stick.

When it is at rest, the hinged part (we could call it the *flap*), will hang downwards to its full extent.

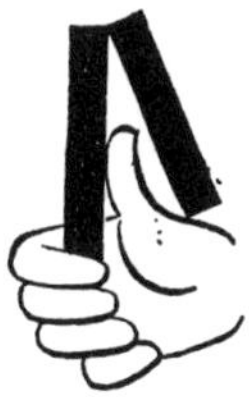

When the hand, which represents an impetus in the direction of the arrow, starts to move, the end of the flap will lift slightly and trail behind as its inertia is overcome.

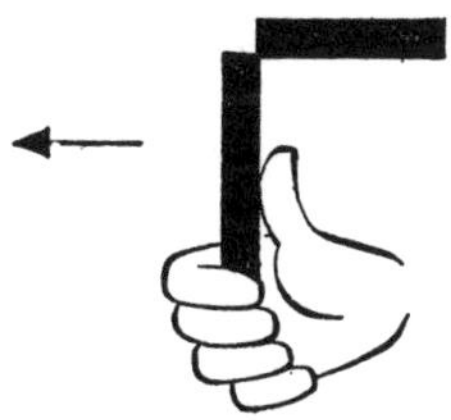

It will continue to rise as the speed increases.

But when the hand with the stick stops, the flap will want to go on moving, and, as it cannot pass the stick, momentum will cause it to rise still further.

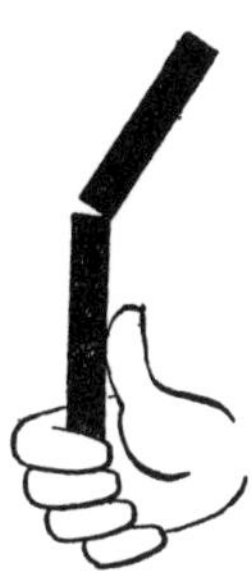

If the hand stopped permanently, the momentum of the flap would be overcome by gravity and it would fall down again, but if the hand changes direction, the upward movement will continue, as momentum is causing the flap to continue moving in the original direction.

Its upper end is being pulled one way, by one force, and its lower end in the opposite way by another force.

So, after the stick has reversed its direction the flap will pass over the top of the stick, fall down on the other side, and remain there until the direction changes again.

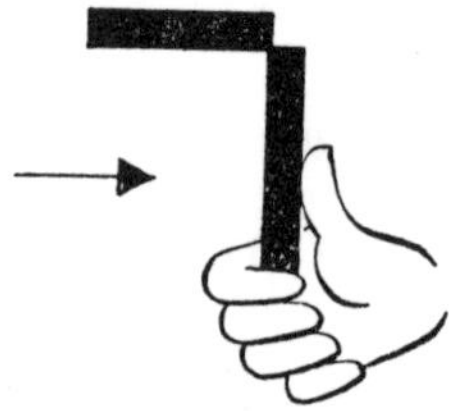

If this movement is animated, it will resemble very closely the distortion which we introduced into the vertical line (p. 36).

There is then, a foundation in nature for the arbitrary distortion which we used merely as an aid to the eye in following movement. So it follows that the more the effects of inertia and momentum are introduced into our animation, the smoother andmor e pleasing it will be.

If this simple hinged stick is used as the basis for the construction of an arm and hand . . .

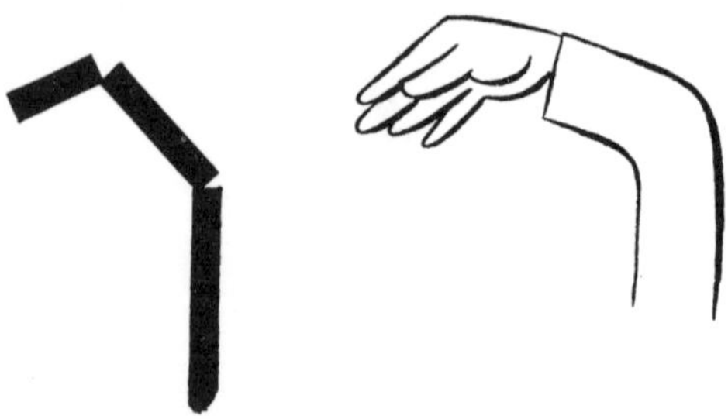

we can see clearly how the principle is applied to the animation of figures.

Remember that the part which has the impetus applied to it will change direction first. Other parts will continue to follow the original direction as long as possible until, in turn, their inertia is overcome.

Animated Waves . . .

There is another effect of this principle which is very easily observed in real life—the waves which appear to run along a length of rope when one end is shaken violently up and down.

The movement of a wave lends itself very definitely to animation, and we can make use of it in many instances with exciting results. It is worth while studying it in detail.

Here is a hand holding the rope.

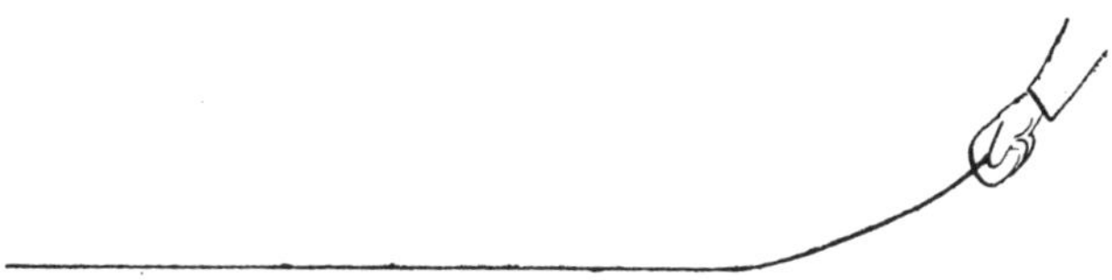

The end is lifted up . . .

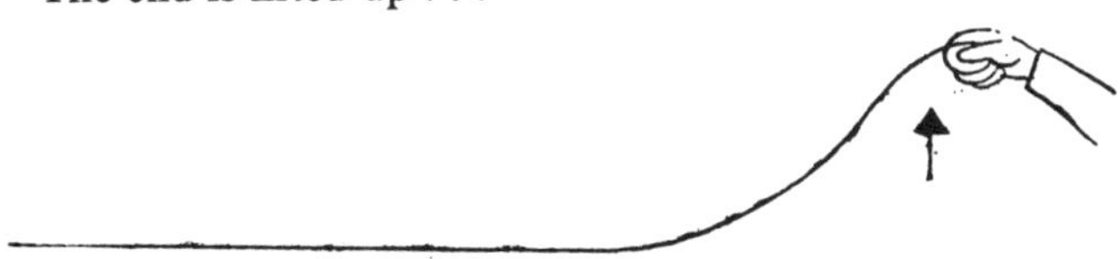

and jerked sharply downwards.

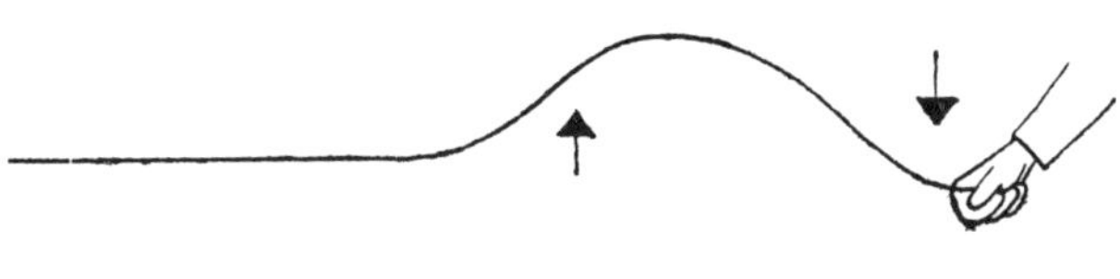

When the second upward movement is started, the momentum is still making part of the rope continue to move downwards . . .

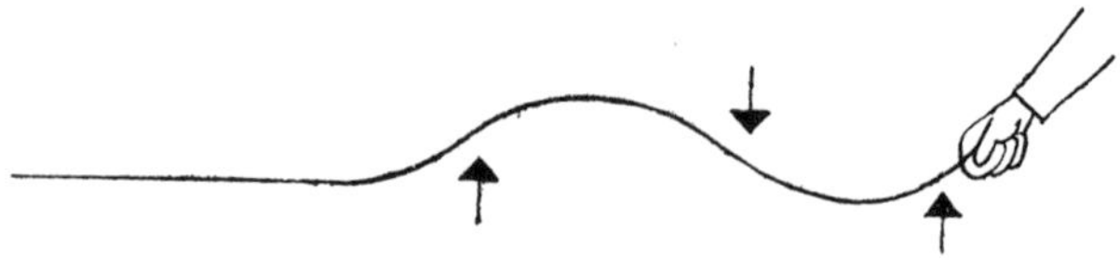

and on the next downward jerk, both the previous upward and downward movements are still going on.

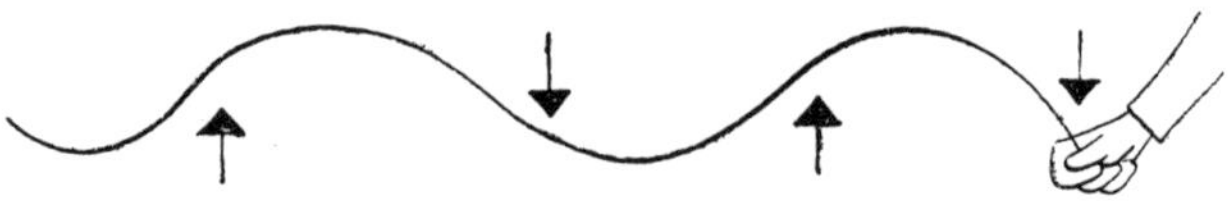

The first wave has now moved along the rope, and others are following it.

When the agitation of the end of the rope is stopped, the last wave will continue to move along until gravity brings it to rest.

When animating this movement, note that there is no intermediate position where the rope is a straight line. In fact, if the experiment is made with a piece of rope, it will be found that considerable force is needed to pull a long rope straight again once a wave system is started in it.

This is because the momentum of the moving rope must be overcome before it can be pulled straight.

In moving a wave crest along then, from A to B, the in-between position must always be at C, the crest moving along a line between the two key positions.

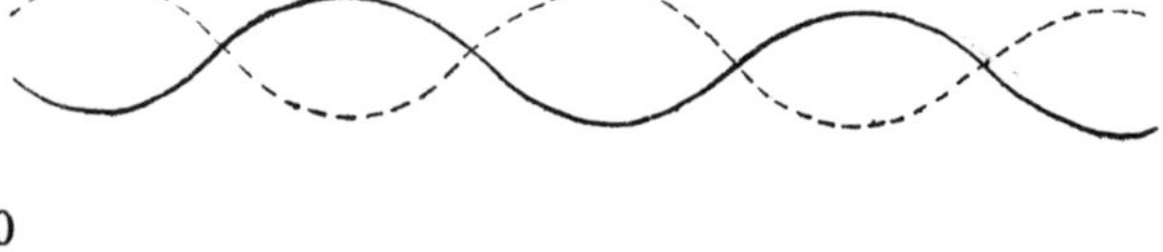

A simple experiment will show the value of this wave movement in animating lines. On a long strip of paper draw a wave . . .

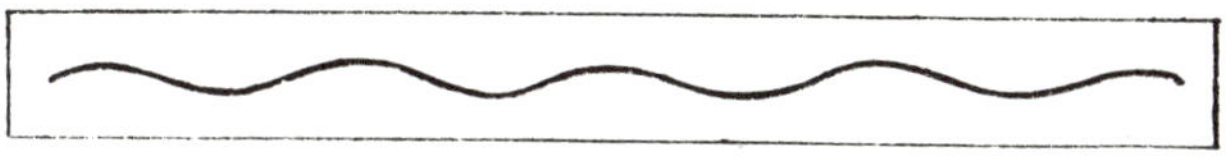

Above this, place another sheet with a small vertical slot in it.

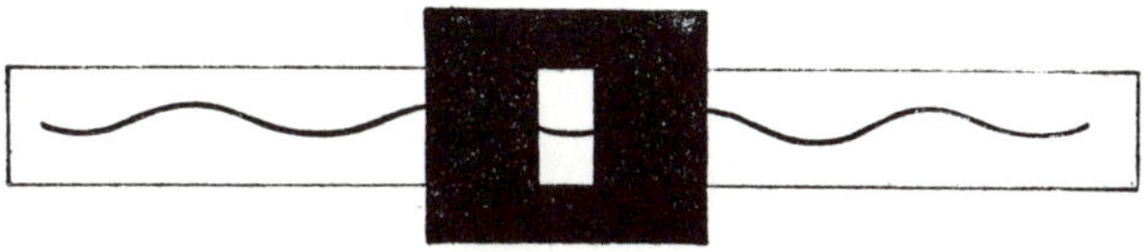

When the strip is pulled from side to side, a line appears to move up and down the slot in a much more attractive way than if it were merely an oscillating straight line.

Always look for opportunities to animate in wave form, as this sort of movement is extremely sympathetic.

. . . *in a Donkey's Tail*

A typical example of the way this movement is used is a donkey waving its tail.

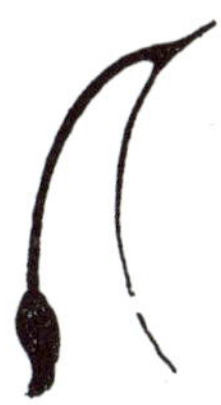

The impetus to lift the tail is given by whatever muscles the donkey uses for this purpose. The inertia of the bobble at the end keeps it hanging downwards while the tail is going up.

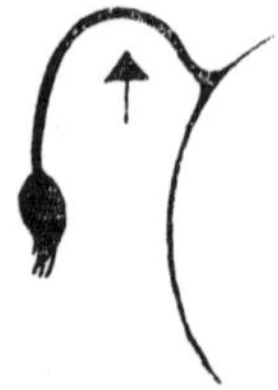

Then the impetus changes direction, the root of the tail moves down, but the momentum of the end still keeps it going up . . .

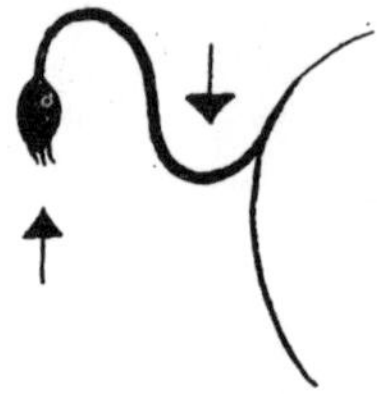

until its momentum is finished.
By this time an upward impetus has started . . .

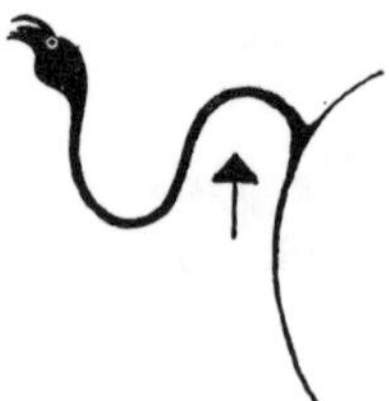

but the bobble is still going down . . .

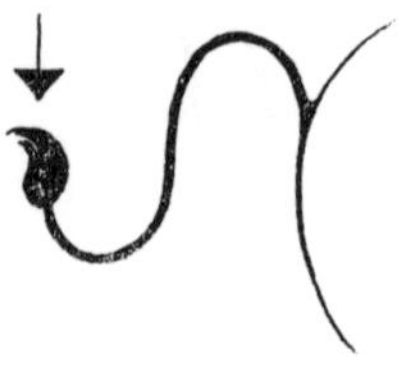

which brings it back to the first key position.

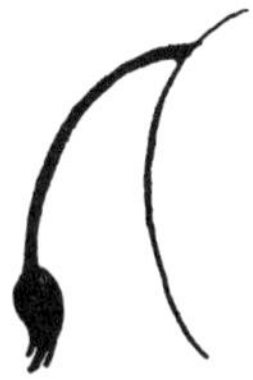

Movements of this kind can be made much more interesting if some perspective is introduced into them. In this case try to make the bobble approach and recede from the camera, giving it a circular motion.

Inertia causes any straight edge of a moving object to curve outwards in the direction of its movement. When the movement is reversed, the straight line curves over in the opposite direction.

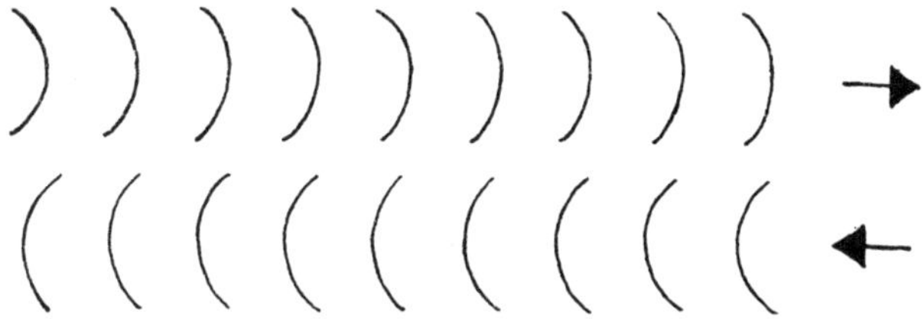

It is better not to draw any intermediate stages of the change over from one curve to another, particularly with fast movement. Then just let the curve snap over.

But if it is necessary to animate the change of curve, always use the wave principle . . .

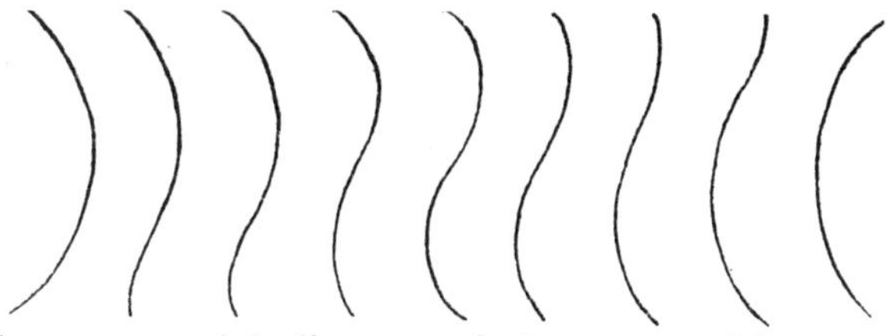

and never a straight line as an in-between position.

Secondary Movements

The last of Newton's rules; the famous one about an equal and opposite reaction, serves to remind us of a way in which we can add emphasis to our movements. We can precede them, accompany them, or follow them by secondary movements in the opposite direction.

A man who is going to dash madly across the screen, will prepare for the big movement forwards by a smaller preliminary movement backwards. . . .

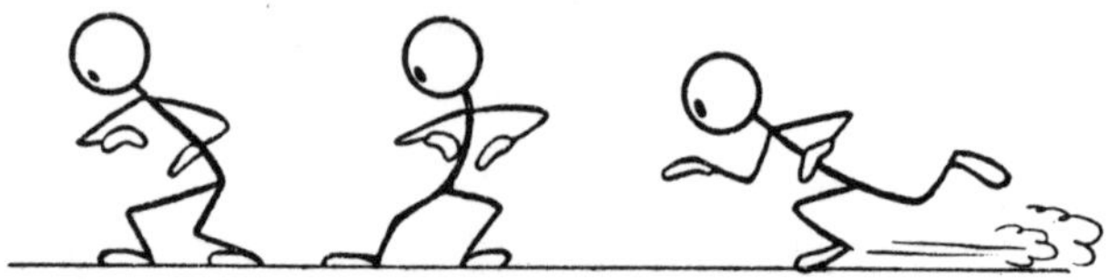

While he is speeding across, the wind of his passage can cause a tree to bend over. . . .

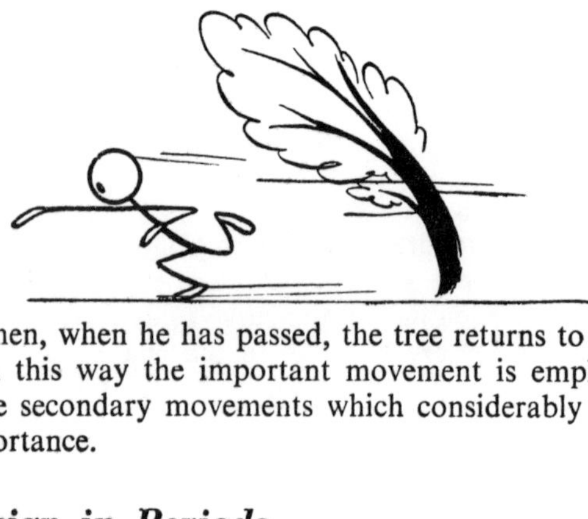

Then, when he has passed, the tree returns to normal.

In this way the important movement is emphasised by three secondary movements which considerably add to its importance.

Design in Periods

A rather common fault in animating a succession of rapid movements is to allow the figures to dash wildly in all directions like mad, without giving the audience a chance to appreciate any individual movement. This often means that a good deal of hard work does not have such a powerful effect on the screen as it deserves.

The mistake can be avoided by always thinking of a movement as having three stages: *anticipation*, *action*, *result*, and allowing for them in the timing.

Anticipation is the preparation for the major movement; a smaller, slower movement in the opposite direction.

Before a jump, the figure crouches.

Before a punch, the fist is drawn back.

Before a dive, the diver stretches up, and poises on his toes.

Then after the major action, comes the effect. There are always opportunities for emphasising the major movement by incidental effects on other objects.

When the man lands on finishing his jump, he will squash; but small objects near him can be made to leap into the air from the impact of his landing.

The diver makes a splash on entering the water, which moves in the opposite direction to him.

In this way, periods of violent movement will be interspersed with periods of quiet, and will gain greatly in effect.

Characters and Script

If we know and understand the three rules of movement, and take every opportunity of making the utmost use of them in animation, we have the fundamentals of all the tricks of the animator's trade.

But there are too many ways in which the effects of these rules, and the distortion they cause in moving objects, can be applied to every kind of character and thing that we can think of. It would be impossible even to attempt to make a list of them.

The best way of getting familiar with all the uses of squash in animation, is to see as many cartoon films as possible, see them again, analyse them, discuss them and criticise them. With the new knowledge we have gained, we shall be able to watch cartoons from an entirely new point of view, and learn something even from the worst of them, if only how *not* to do it.

Continue to practise and experiment with animation, attempting more and more ambitious subjects and movements. The moment will soon come when you feel that it would not be a complete waste of time and film to set out on a full scale production of your own.

How do we start?

Our Actors . . .

First we shall need characters.

The little pin figures we have been using during the practising period have several advantages. The chief one is that they are very easy to draw, and so save a great deal of work. In fact it is quite possible to make extremely entertaining little films with pin people as the only characters, moving in very simple surroundings designed to suit them. They are capable of expressing many kinds of emotions by movement (which is the only way of expressing emotion in cartoon), and can be made to stretch and squash in any way required.

Also they will teach us an economy of design and expression which will be very useful when we finally desert them for more fully developed and intricate characters.

But remember that every line added to a character is equivalent to a definite number of hours of work added to the production time of the film. You will have to make up your minds whether this additional work is repaid by additional pictorial and emotional value on the screen. The result can be judged only by the action that appears on the screen.

You cannot justify an unsuccessful film by pointing to an individual drawing and saying, "But look how beautiful this is!"

. . . *Take Shape*

Cartoon characters must be designed so that they can be imagined and drawn in every possible position in space, quickly and easily, and by all the members of the team, if there is one, working on the film.

They must, therefore, be built up of simple, solid, geometrical shapes, and have fixed proportions that can easily be recognised and reproduced, no matter what size the character is to be drawn.

They must also be capable of being stretched, squashed and distorted to an enormous extent without losing the original underlying shape.

Very few of us would be able to draw a skull, for instance, quickly and clearly, from above, below and sideways. It would be almost impossible to stretch a skull to three times its length, or squash it as flat as a penny, and still keep it recognisable as a skull.

But we have all done this quite easily with a ball. A sphere remains a sphere from which ever angle it is looked at. And no matter how drastically it is distorted, it never loses its essential character. So the sphere is a better basis for designing our cartoon people than something so intricate as, say, a skull.

Simple Shapes . . .

Two balls joined together make an ovoid shape which can easily be bent in the middle. This makes an excellent body, both human and animal.

Variations of character can be made by varying the sizes of the balls. This also applies to the head.

The arms and legs can be cylinders, either one bent in the middle, or two of different sizes hinged at the elbow or knee.

Hands and feet are flat discs, with the fingers or toes, small cylinders, attached to them.

With such simple shapes as the sphere, the cylinder, the cone and the disc, of varying proportions, an infinite variety of characters can be built up.

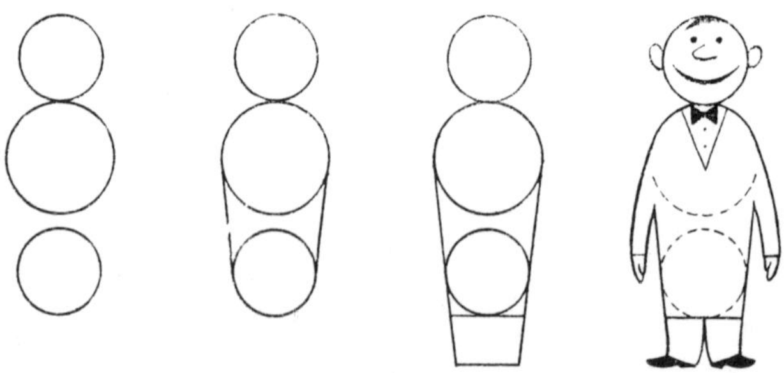

Always think of the characters as being built of *solid* shapes. They will, of course, be drawn flat, but to think of them as solid while they are being drawn and animated helps to make them look solid on the screen.

These underlying solid shapes, too, are disguised to a certain extent when the detail of the character is completed, but they should always be roughed in first when drawing so that their presence is felt in the solidity of the character.

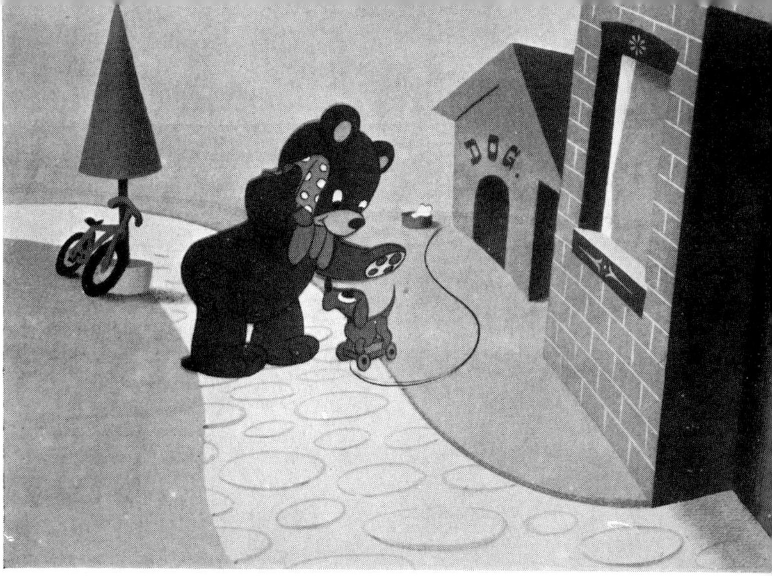

These two illustrations are from "Dolly put the Kettle on" and "Fly about the House", both professionally produced cartoons. The running time of the former is 2 minutes. It requires 1,100 celluloids and animation and 25 painted backgrounds. The latter required 4,700 celluloids and 82 backgrounds.

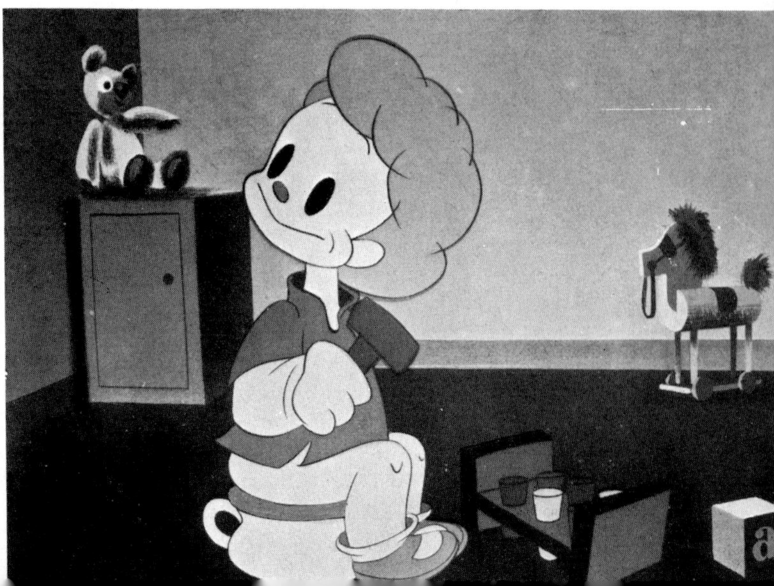

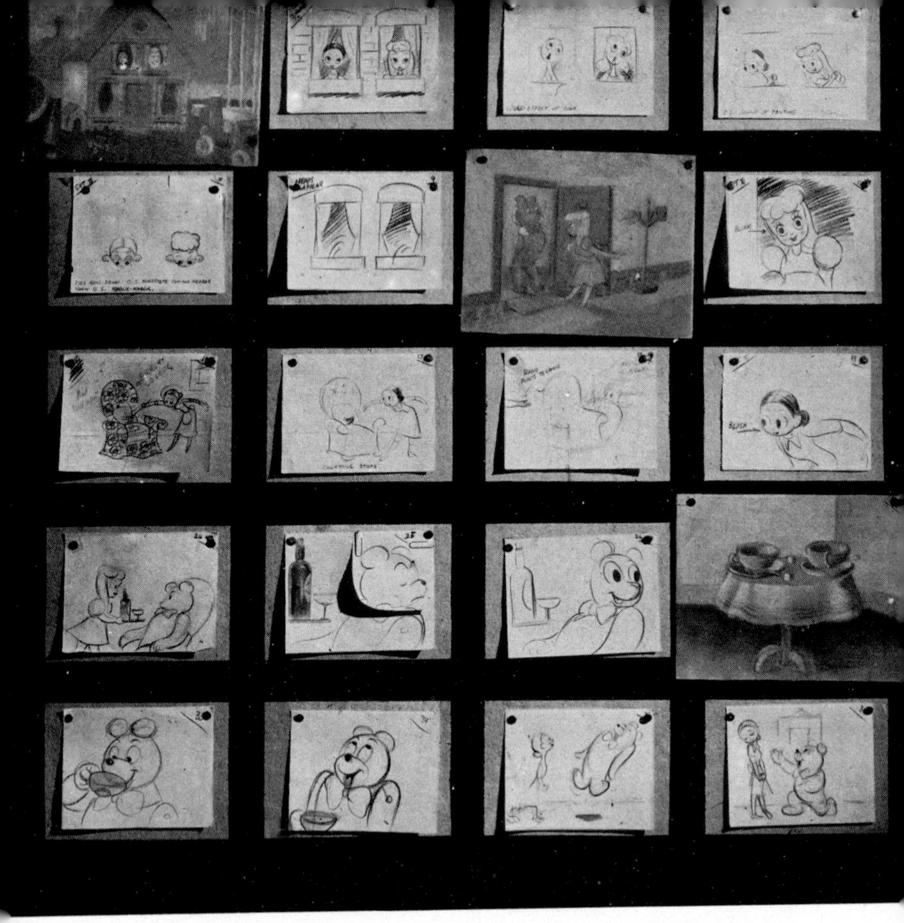

Story board of "Dolly put the Kettle on". While this story board technique is a "must" in a professional cartoon studio, it is also very useful in other kinds of production. If you want to be sure of the smooth continuity of your story, there is no better way to ensure it than to preconceive it with some rough sketches. Cartoon, more than any other type of film making, can pre-select its situations, camera set-ups and editing. So don't leave to chance what your figures will do and how your objects will appear on the screen. Rough them out in small

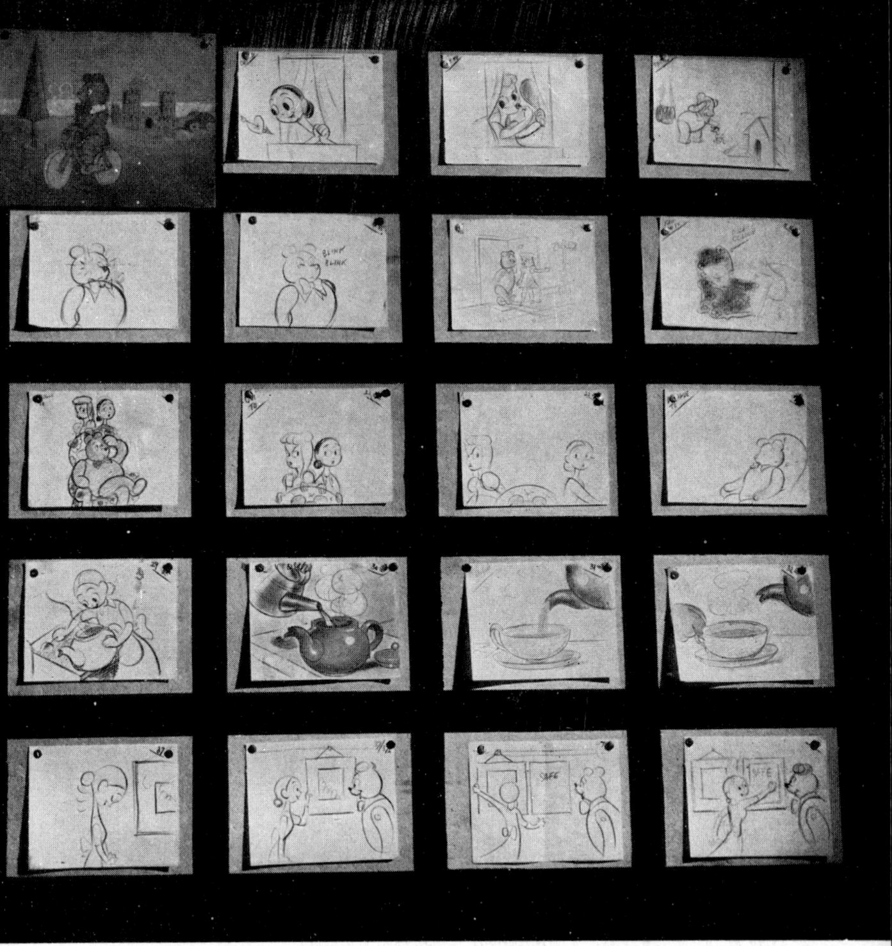

thumb-nail sketches, concentrating mainly on (a) whether the drawings express the film's main idea clearly and smoothly, (b) whether one shot follows the other, smoothly, which, of course, will depend on how the angles of shots and the sizes of figures were chosen. The design and the tones of the background, the tones or the colour of the figures, could be worked out within the story board too. What the blue-print is to a building project, the story board is to the cartoon.

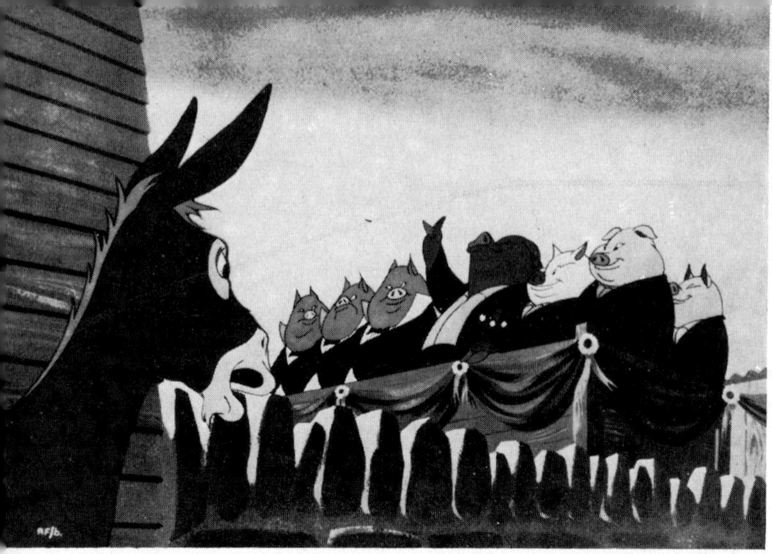

Stills from "Animal Farm" and "History of the Cinema", both professionally produced cartoons. The first film, 75 minutes in length, required 250,000 drawings and the latter, 10 minutes in length required 11,000 drawings. The flat surface of the moving figures blends well with the background employing half tones or several shades of colour.

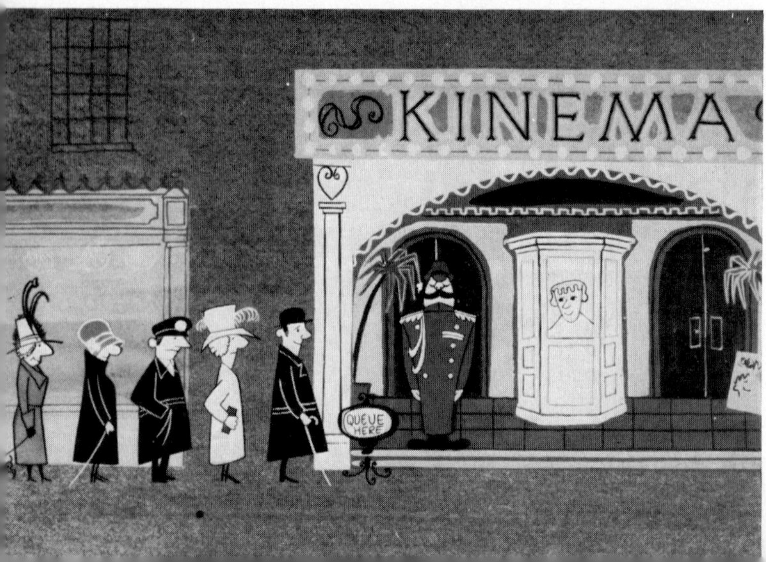

The simplest type of head is a ball. As this turns, either sideways or up and down, the features will appear to revolve round it.

The most prominent feature is the nose, so this must be a separate shape—a little pyramid or cone, or a ball of varying size.

An animal's snout is another small ball which revolves round the larger ball which is his head.

The mouth is a line, when closed, which becomes a concave depression of varying size and shape when open.
The eyes are considered as flat shapes painted on.

. . . *Become Personalities*

When we are sufficiently adept at building figures with the building blocks of our imagination, we must turn them into characters.

Cartoon characters should be broadly and very clearly defined. They should be the essence of the type they represent. We simplify characters and attributes just as we did with their shapes.

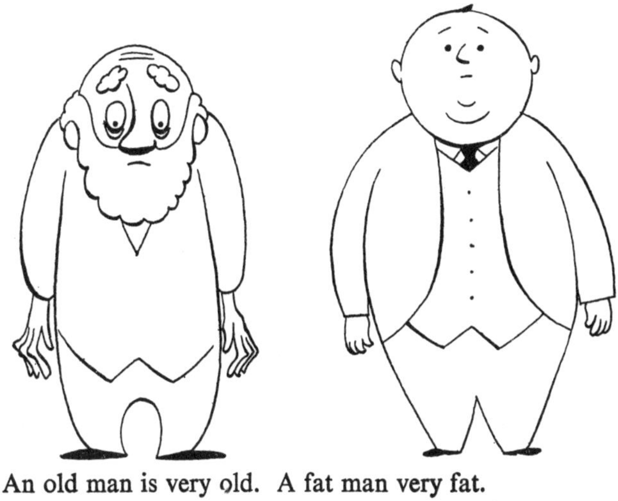

An old man is very old. A fat man very fat.

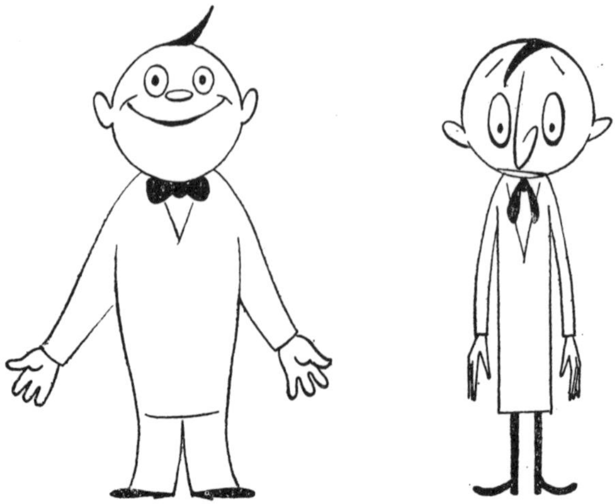

A happy man is bursting with joy. A sad man is the epitome of melancholy.

It is very difficult to express the middle way in a cartoon: it is usually either all or nothing.

As soon as you have decided on each character, make a chart showing his proportions.

The length of the head is usually taken as the unit of measurement.

Draw the character in full face, profile and three-quarters view, with the proportions of his salient divisions clearly marked in multiples or fractions of the length of the head.

It is a good idea to make a separate chart of the head, squared up to show the position of the features, as these have a tendency to slip out of place when the figure is animated.

If a character is drawn several hundred times over, the construction must be simple enough to avoid unwanted distortion.

Economy demands simplicity too. A character based on complicated lines will cost more and take far longer to animate than a simple one.

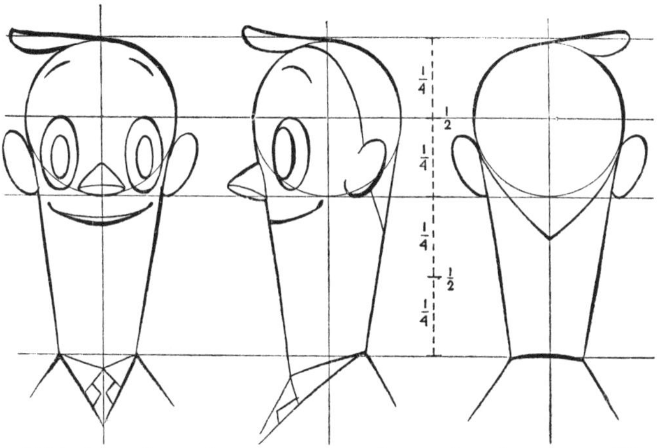

This is a chart showing proportions of a character. The unit of measurement here is half the length of the head. The proportions and position of the features are clearly established. If animation drawings are constantly compared with the chart, the animator will soon be able to draw the figure instinctively in any position, and distort him in any way without losing the essential character.

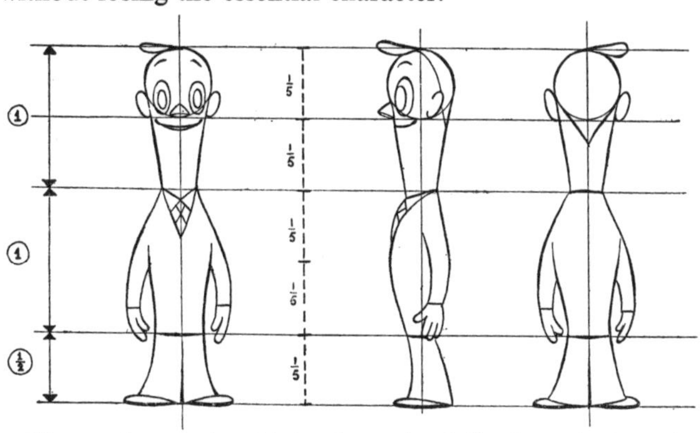

These charts should be kept in full view during the production of the film.

The Story is Planned . . .

The general idea of the story our characters are going to act is then expanded into the *shooting script.*

This should be as comprehensive as we can possibly make it, giving the whole of the action divided into separate scenes, including details of the background against which each scene will be played.

The imagined position and angle of the camera in relation to the characters, and any change of position of the camera during the scene should be noted.

The method to be used in changing from one scene to the next must be indicated and the complete timing of every action worked out in detail.

If we are making a sound film, the script should contain a column where sound effects, music and dialogue are described in the correct position where they will occur.

If the script is correctly and fully prepared, it should be possible for any member of the team working on the film to choose a scene anywhere in the film, design it and animate it so that it will fit smoothly into the rest.

The script is the framework on which the film is built, and production should not start until it has been thoroughly discussed, criticised and amended by all the members of the team.

. . . in Terms of Action

The theme of the story should be as simple as possible, and be one that can be expressed by action alone.

Any situations where the characters are inclined to remain still, or where only limited movement is possible, should be avoided.

In a sound film, humour of the conversational type is extremely difficult to portray, so dialogue should be reduced to an absolute minimum.

In a silent film titles should be used as little as possible, as they interrupt the flow of the action.

But though the actors should be kept moving, the story

should allow for variations in the speed of the movement.

It should contain possibilities for both rapid and slow action, and the gags should arise directly from the action, and not dragged in where they don't fit naturally.

Don't let it be overloaded with gags and ideas. Carefully prune and select them, allow time for each to be worked out to give the maximum effect, and save the rest for another film.

A common weakness of first efforts is that they tend to get crowded with all the ideas of a lifetime.

The Story Must Run Smoothly

The next problem is to divide the script into scenes.

Here the question of *continuity*, the changing from one scene to another, will arise.

The cartoon director cannot employ the method frequently adopted by the live action director: shooting an excess of material from different angles and distances, and then experimenting with the many different ways of assembling and editing the material until the best result is obtained. We cannot afford to animate a scene both in mid shot and close up, and decide afterwards which one to use. So our editing must be visualised at the scripting stage.

To help us in this, each scene should be illustrated by rough sketches, made as the script is being prepared.

If these are assembled in order, and arranged on a large board, the *story board*, it is much easier to criticise and amend the script. Afterwards they can be used as a basis for the final layout drawings for each scene.

When discussing the script as it appears on the story board, we must painstakingly visualise the whole film, its settings, characters and tempo from the point of view of the audience.

Continuity is not simply a matter of ensuring that a character appears in the same clothes in two consecutive scenes.

It is essential to the smooth unfolding of the story; so

that the audience know where they are, and what they are looking at at any point in the film.

Is the close up recognisable from the medium or long shot preceding it?

Should this close up be before or after that long shot?

Does the man turn right or left when he comes out of the door, if he is walking along the road from left to right in the next shot from the opposite angle?

Are the characters easily recognisable, or will there be confusion as to who is which?

Are we allowing enough time for this situation to be understood?

Can we speed up, or omit altogether, this bit of action?

Is this effect worth the work we'll have to put into it?

Which are the high points of the story needing emphasis?

Many questions like these will have to be answered before the story board is passed and animation can start. It is false to leave them to be solved during production. That will only land you in a muddle.

If the action of the whole story takes place in a compact setting, such as a house, and its immediate surroundings, it is a good idea to make a rough model from which the camera angles are worked out. This will probably give you more ideas for imaginative compositions and angles, and it will be easier to check that the camera does not take violent leaps, but follows the action smoothly from one place to another.

The art of continuity can best be learnt, again, by studying other people's work, seeing as many cartoon films as possible, since in fundamentals the problems and methods are always the same.

Scenes Must be Linked Up

The way in which shots are linked together, also has an important bearing on continuity and must be planned in the script.

The various methods are somewhat analogous to the

punctuation marks in a text: full stop, semi-colon, paragraph, etc.

We can have:

1. The *cut*. This is the comma of a film sequence. Here the first frame of the action of one scene follows directly after the last frame of the previous scene. It is the most frequently used and the most effective method of giving pace to the film.

   Always cut on action, that is, keep the movement going right to the last frame of the scene, and from the first frame of the next.

   Never freeze the movement and then cut.

   Avoid double action; movement at the end of one scene repeated in the next.

2. The *mix*, or a *cross dissolve*. Here one scene fades in at the same time as the previous one is fading out.

   If the cut is a comma, the mix may be a full stop, and begins a new sentence.

   The length of a mix is variable, but the best time is 1 second. It can be longer or shorter than this, according to the length of time necessary for the pause for breath between sentences.

   Again it is advisable to keep movement going during a mix, but not as essential as in cutting.

3. *Fade out* and *fade in*. One scene fades to black and the next fades in from black.

   This is the end of one paragraph, or chapter, and the beginning of the next.

4. *Panning* and *tracking* shots. These are changes of scene more slowly than by cutting, effected by movement of the camera.

   In panning (*pan* is a contraction of *panorama*) the camera turns from side to side, a horizontal pan; in moving it up and down, we have a vertical pan—a tilt.

   In cartoons, this is achieved by movement of the background. The latter is drawn longer than the size of field, and slides along a small distance for every frame.

Tracking is the movement of the camera towards or away from the field.

5. *Wipes*. The scene appears to slide over another one.

   This may happen from side to side, up or down, expanding from any point in screen, or contracting from outside. In fact, the dividing line between the two scenes can be of any shape.

   Wipes should be used with great economy, but are often most effective if used imaginatively for a special purpose. They also are like a mix, equivalent to a full stop; the end of one sentence and beginning of the next one.

6. *Iris*. This is frequently used at the end of a cartoon film.

   A circle surrounded by solid black is animated to close in from outside the screen. It can centre on any point within the field.

   Alternatively, a black circle can expand from any point until the whole screen is covered.

   A combination of these two methods is a useful substitute for a mix or a wipe.

   Another use of the iris is to emphasise any action which does not occupy the whole screen without cutting to close up. An iris can partly close in to surround the action, framing it in black.

However, straightforward and simple continuity is usually better than clever tricks. Skilful cutting increases the tempo of the film. Fast action is emphasised if it is divided into a series of scenes, getting shorter as the climax is reached. Mixing slows down the tempo. Cutting makes photography easier. Several scenes connected by mixes makes it necessary to shoot many feet of film at one time. If anything goes wrong in one scene, the whole lot will have to be re-taken. So don't use mixes or wipes unless they are necessary to bridge a gap in time or space.

And Now a Complete Script

This is what the first of your labours should look like. It's quite a simple effort, taking just 1 minute on the screen.

SING A SONG OF SIXPENCE

	Action	*Secs.*	*Frames*	*Music and Effects*
1.	*Fade in.*	2	48	
	Attic room. *Hold* on the picture of the master, the old man, on the wall and calendar showing Friday (pay day) the 13th.	2	48	
	Track and *pan away.*	2	48	Accent for waking the dog.
	To include dog sleeping (at end dog suddenly wakes).	4	96	
2.	Closer shot of dog listening.	2	48	Creaking footsteps approaching.
3.	Shot of door. Door opens revealing the old man.	1	24	
	Dog rushes at him.	1	24	
	Wipe to.	1	24	
4.	Old man on his chair.			
	He takes a bone, gives it to dog.	1	24	
	Dog eats it, from other pocket man takes out a battered purse.	1	24	
	Looks suspiciously round.	1	24	
5.	Closer shot, old man transfers the contents of purse to the old stocking.	1	24	
	Puts it under pillow.	1	24	
	Pats pillow.	1	24	
	Wipe to night shot.	1	24	
	The two retire to rest.	1	24	
	Mix to.	1	24	
	Outside of house.	1	24	
6.	Candle light disappears (on 25th frame after mix).	1	24	
	Lettering jumps in.			
	"Some hours later" (*Hold* and lettering jumps out).	2	48	
	Silence.	1	24	
	Suddenly flames burst from the lower storey and spread very rapidly.	1	24	
	Flames spreading.	2	48	Noise of dog barking madly. Fire engine. Flames sizzling.
	Sheet comes down.	½	12	
	Old man descends.	2½	60	
7.	Old man sits still, huddles in the gutter.	1	24	Accent.

	Action	*Secs.*	*Frames*	*Music and Effects.*
	The image of his stocking appears over his head (*Hold*).	1	24	
	The image of his beloved dog with halo appears on the other side (*Hold*).	1	24	Accent.
	The images dissolve.	1	24	
	Mix to.	1	24	
	Dog with lively step and triumphant expression walks along with the stocking in his mouth.	4	96	Very lively music.
8.	*Long shot*, dog arrives at a Post Office.	4	96	
9.	*Closer shot*, dog in front of Post Office just settles down on the doorsteps.	2	96	
	Pan and track up to name plate.	2	96	
	Hold name plate "Post Office Savings Bank 8.30—6.30."	3	72	
	Mix in end title "Better Save than Sorry".	1	24	
	Hold end title.	3	72	
	Fade out.	1	24	Play out.

Making Things Easier

The aim of anybody making a cartoon film, unless he has unlimited resources at his disposal, should be to achieve the maximum possible effect for the minimum amount of work. This is important right from the earliest stages of the preparation of the script.

Less Drawing with the Same Effect

Choose scenes which offer possibilities of reducing the number of animation drawings.

Abandon scenes which can only be successful if a large amount of work is put into them, unless they are absolutely essential to the film. Simplicity is especially essential in television films. No complicated animation or over-elaborate backgrounds are noticeable on a small television screen.

The amount of work necessary for each drawing must be taken into account in designing the characters, and every unnecessary line ruthlessly excluded. Even Walt Disney has found that lions come cheaper than tigers; lions don't have stripes to be drawn and painted over and over again!

The average number of animation drawings for one second of screen time indicates the amount of work involved. So if we wish to cut down the work to reasonable limits, we must look for ways of reducing this average.

There are many ways of doing this. But such ways of "cheating" must not become obvious on the screen.

Making One Picture do the Work of Several

The most frequently used method has already been described—animation at double frame. It is always advisable to line test all animation, except the fastest movements, at double frame first, and only add the single in-between drawings if double frame is not successful.

Another device already mentioned is the repeating movement, where the last key drawing is also the first, and the action can be repeated many times with the same drawings.

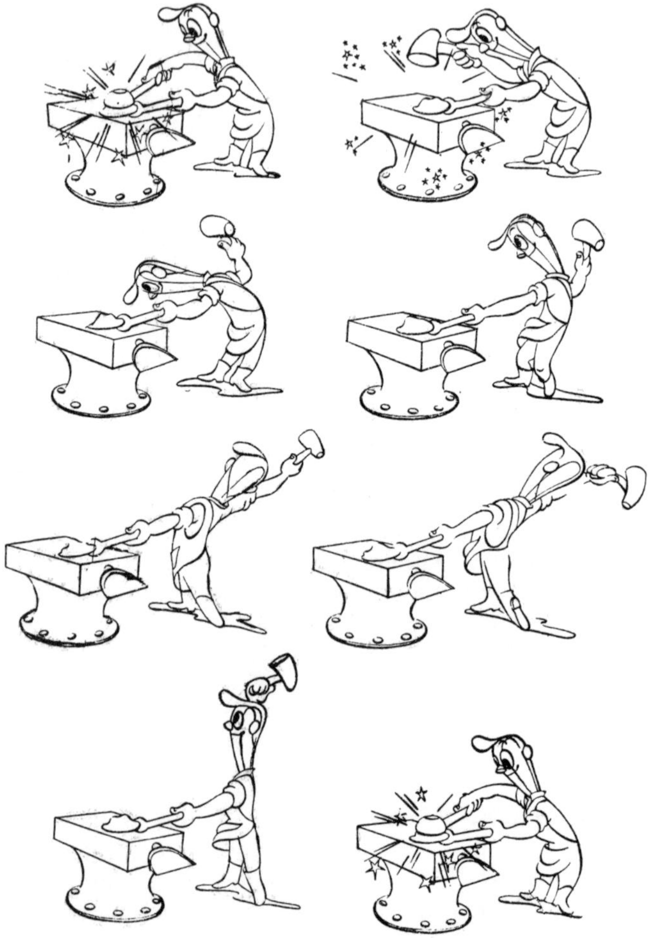

To increase the variety, two repeats of the same action can be animated with slight variations. These repeats are then alternated if the movement has to go on for a considerable time.

Economy in the Background . . .

Walking or running when the figure is not in perspective, can be made into a repeat by assuming that the camera is panning to follow the moving character, keeping him in the centre of the screen.

Instead of moving across the screen, our little man will walk in the same place, his feet sliding backwards during the time they are in contact with the ground. If the background is calibrated to move the same distance that his foot moves backward in every frame, he will, in fact, seem to move forward.

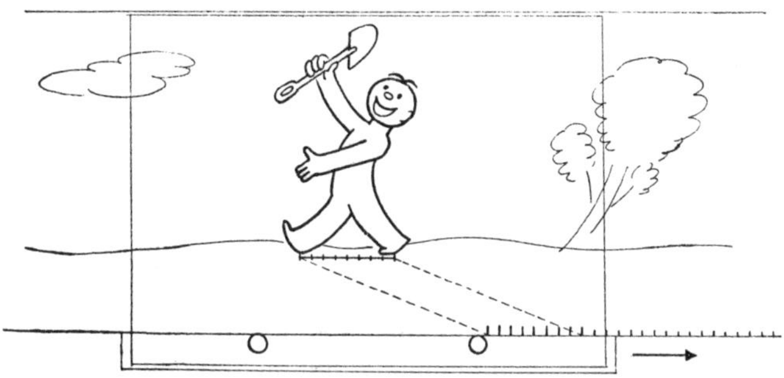

The same thing can be done with an object such as a motor car. The jolting up and down movement of the car is animated (in a very exaggerated way) as a repeat, together with the rotation of the wheels and the puffing of the exhaust. The background slides in the opposite direction.

For fast movement like this, the background should not be sharply drawn. Instead, the outlines in the background have blurred edges on the side away from the direction of movement.

A figure can be made to walk right across the screen by repeating drawings.

The animation is done in the same way as for a panning walk, his feet slipping backwards (p. 85). Then the drawings are traced on long sheets of paper, or celluloid (if it is used) which rest against (but are not put over) the register pegs. These sheets are of sufficient length to ensure that they cover the whole field when the character is outside the field of view at either side.

Take the first key drawing, No. 1, and put it against the pegs so that the front foot is on the ground, just inside the frame. Mark this position with a line at the bottom of the paper just opposite the centre of one of the pegs.

Then place drawing No. 2 above it, so that the foot that is on the ground is in the same position as the same foot in drawing No. 1. Mark this position and continue in the same way with all the drawings until he has walked as far as necessary.

Each drawing will be used a number of times, but

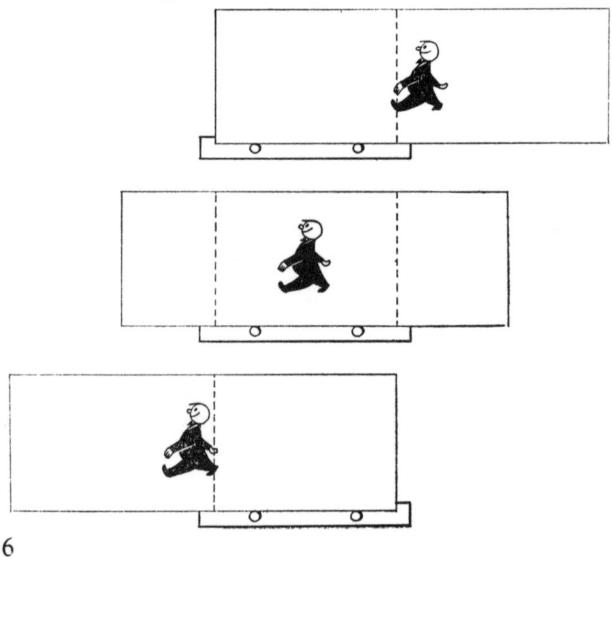

each time it will be advanced by the length of one step.

A more complicated, but sometimes also more effective variation is to move the background backward at half speed while the figure moves forward at half speed.

This method is also used when we pan the camera away from one scene to direct it on the next. The animation is traced on long sheets of paper, and each drawing in turn is moved a stage away from the direction the camera is assumed to be moving. The background, of course, also moves in the same direction, but not so fast, as it is further away (see p. 41).

. . . *in Perspective* . . .

Movement in perspective can also be made into a repeat by animating both the character and the background.

This time we have to imagine that the camera is travelling along in front of the moving character, and remaining the same distance away from him.

The background is kept very simple, and must be designed with straight or curved lines receding into the distance to emphasise the perspective. Along these lines there should be a series of regularly spaced simple objects, such as stones, trees or telegraph poles, drawn in perspective, getting smaller and closer together in the distance.

We then animate a repeat of these objects moving in the opposite direction to the movement of the figure. Each of the objects is animated on until it takes the place of the next in the line.

When this is combined with the repeat animation of the figure walking or running, but remaining in the same place in the frame we have a very effective shot.

. . . *and in Scripting*

Apart from such cycles of movements, whole sequences of action can often be repeated. Many gags can be worked out by repeating actions several times.

The basis of them is as a rule something like this.

A man does certain things with a certain result, usually painful. He tries again, same result. He then sees that if he does it differently, he will avoid the inevitable consequence. He does so, successfully the first time. But later on circumstances have changed, and the result happens just the same, if not worse. And so on.

But don't make the mistake of thinking that if a thing is funny, or dramatic when it happens once, it will have twice the effect if it happens twice. This is sometimes the case, but certainly not always.

Action can often be planned to take place off the screen altogether, thus avoiding animation of it completely. If this is done with imagination, the audience will possibly refrain from demanding their money back.

As an example, let us imagine two men who are going to fight. One takes a tentative blow, and the other returns it. Pan away from them, using this same animation on long sheets of paper. The combatants are now outside the frame area. Continue the pan, and bring in a small boy, sitting on a gate, nonchalantly munching a large sandwich, and looking out of the frame towards the fight. For emphasis, clouds of dust can puff in from this direction. Cut to the two contestants, very battered, in whatever situation is necessary for the continuation of the story.

By taking trouble, in the scripting stage, to work out shots of this sort, we may save a considerable amount of work, and the result is often better than it would have been if we used more labour but less imagination.

Repeated cycles can often be made to continue far longer, and be less obvious, if they are *intercut* or alternated with other scenes. This also increases the pace of the film.

To take an easy example, suppose our subject is a burlesque of a melodrama, and the humour is derived from deliberate "corn".

The heroine is bound to the rails, and the express is approaching. (This is merely an example of a method, and not of good scripting!)

We have animated two shots of the train, and have put a considerable amount of work into it. One, perhaps, shows it approaching the camera round a bend, and the other is a top shot with the train going diagonally across our field view.

Trace both these shots in reverse, and make alternative backgrounds for them. The same animation has now been extended into four different scenes, each of which can be on the screen for several seconds. They can then be repeated, if they are intercut with shots (they could even be stills), of such things as a signal; the heroine in close up and medium shot; the villain and the hero. Imaginative cutting can be the best possible labour saver.

If our camera is capable of tracking, we can save ourselves a good deal of work. The same animation can look quite different if is repeated in close up.

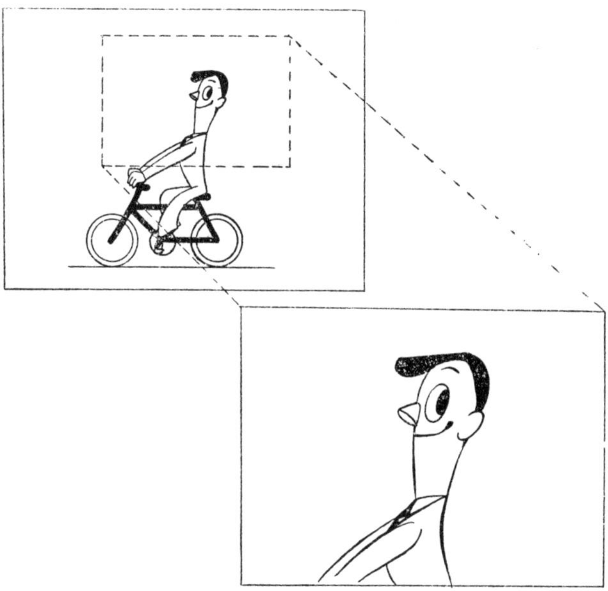

We can make a very complicated object, such as an aeroplane, move up right to the camera by tracking in on it against a featureless background.

And at least once in a film we can work in a *location shot* where the camera pans and tracks up on a still background for several seconds, without any animation at all.

Additional atmosphere can be given to shots of this sort by the animation of shadows. Sometimes we can turn aside from the movement of the characters to watch the movement of their shadows. A complete fantasy can be developed from shadows only.

There is no limit to the ways of reducing the number of drawings, and the amount of time and labour, without in any way reducing the quality of the film. We can adapt these methods, and many others that will occur to us as we become more experienced in a hundred different ways. The right time to think of them is the scripting stage of the film so that we don't have to interrupt production by making amendments to the script. Sometimes, particularly with our first films, we may find we can't avoid that altogether. But all the same, the less script work is needed during production, the better.

If, as is quite possible, we can reduce the average number of drawings per second to about six, a fast moving and well-animated cartoon, lasting about four minutes is not such a herculean task as it may seem.

Producing the Cartoon

In a professional studio there are quite a few stages between the completion of the script, the story sketches and the start of the actual production of the film.

But just let us see what happens there.

Teamwork Counts

The composer is briefed about the type of music required, and uses the time-script as the basis for the rhythm and moods of his music.

Meanwhile the layout and colour design of every scene is put in hand, and more finished drawings are prepared from which the animators and background artists will eventually work.

The music and dialogue is then recorded onto the film.

Before the animation can start, the music must be very carefully analysed, so that movements can be synchronised with it. The number of frames to each bar of music is counted and a detailed chart made of them.

This chart is showing the position in the bar of separate notes of the melody and orchestration, the exact position to a

"CHARLEY SIGNATURE TUNE" (BARS 7–15) 8 SECONDS.

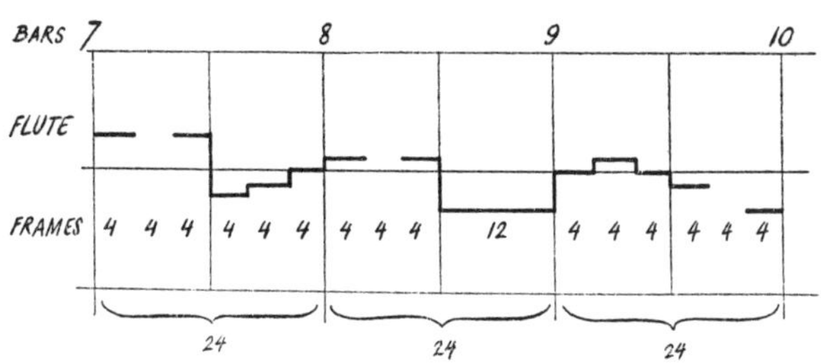

single frame of all accented notes and other details of the music.

These charts are passed to the animators who, with the help of the music charts, are able to prepare and number the key drawings.

When the animation is completed and photographed, and projected together with the sound track, the action should develop on the beat of the music.

The animators also prepare designs and details of the backgrounds, which are passed to the background artists for completion in colour.

At the same time another chart, the camera chart, is made for the guidance of the camera man in photographing the scene.

The Pictures are Built Up . . .

By the time the animation reaches the camera room, the drawings will have been traced on to transparent sheets of plastic material, the cells, and painted in colour or tone.

Each moving figure or object has a series of cells to itself, so that one figure can remain still while another is moving; or one can move at double frame while another is moving at single frame.

So each frame is built up of several layers. First comes the background, above it the cells containing the moving objects, and possibly a cut out foreground behind which the characters pass.

The camera chart gives complete details of this complicated process; it indicates any panning movements of the background, the order of the cells placed above it, and details of what cells must be changed for each frame.

It also describes what camera movements are to take place in tracking, any change in the position of the register pegs, and the length and position of mixes, fades, wipes and other special effects.

Without it, the situation would be completely out of control, so its accurate preparation is a very important part of the animator's work.

. . . *from Initial Keys* . . .

The animator frequently makes his *keys* in rough, and they may be as far apart in time as one second, or even more, leaving a large number of in-between drawings to be put in.

They are taken over by another artist, the assistant animator, who is responsible for cleaning up and breaking down. He makes finished drawings from the key animator's roughs, and reduces the gaps between them by making other drawings at closer stages.

Then the in-between artist completes the process.

The pencil drawings are photographed, with a roughly indicated background, drawn on cell, placed over them so that a *line test* of the complete scene can be viewed on the screen, criticised by the director, altered if necessary, and line tested again until it is considered to be as good as it ever will be.

The editor assembles the line test film of each scene, and matches it to the sound track, so that the director can see how the whole film is progressing, and make alterations to the continuity, camera view points and so on, before it is too late.

The *line test cutting copy*, as it is called, is finally used as a guide to the assembly of the finished scenes as they are received from the processing laboratory.

. . . *to the Final Animation*

After the line tests have been passed, the scene goes to the tracing department.

Here, each drawing in turn is placed on the register pegs, a punched sheet of cell placed over it, and a careful tracing made in ink or poster colour.

If an "actor" passes behind an object on the background, the tracer is responsible for registering the figure to the background so that no gap will show when both are on the pegs under the camera.

The tracing department also checks the camera charts made by the animators.

The final stage is the painting, when the tracer's outlines are filled in with the required colour in oil paint. The paint is applied on the reverse side of the cell, so as not to disturb the tracing line. Great care must be taken to put the paint on smoothly, without lumps which will cause it to crack when pressed down under the camera. It is also very important that the paint in each space of the same colour is of exactly the same tone and colour on each cell, and has no marks or scratches. Otherwise a very unpleasant flicker will occur on the screen.

After a final check, the complete scene, background and camera chart is passed to the camera room for photography.

Our Means may be Limited

This is, of course, a far cry from the amateur's way of doing things.

Unless he has very considerable resources in time and money, the amateur film cartoonist will have to simplify this complicated process. But he can still obtain a result on the screen which will not fall far short of professional standards.

The biggest item in the cost of materials is the sheets of celluloid or plastic, which at the present time are expensive and not always easy to obtain in quantity. So if a method can be found to eliminate the use of cell as far as possible, costs will be very greatly reduced.

This can be done by going back to the technique used by the pioneers of animated film. In the days of "Mutt and Jeff" and the immortal "Felix the Cat", animation on cell was the rare exception rather than the general rule it is to-day.

The animation was done on white paper, the characters being drawn in black and white, without half tones, black predominating.

If more than one level of animation was needed, as we now use several levels of cell, holes were cut in the sheets of paper of the upper drawings so that those beneath showed through. In some cases it was necessary to cut right round a drawing, leaving only a narrow strip of paper connecting it to the pegs.

The background was drawn on a sheet of cell, and placed *over* the animation drawings. As the greater part of the figures was filled in with solid black, it did not matter if they overlapped the lines in the background. Though if a clear part of a figure had to be superimposed over a detail of the background, the background line was scraped off the cell, and drawn in again in the next position after the figure had moved past.

These early films were admittedly comparatively crude judged by modern standards; and, of course, it is by modern standards that our productions will be judged. So, if we adopt the early technique, we must make sure that we do not also reproduce the early crudities and failings. However, these did not arise, in the main, from the technique used, but from design, story and animation.

Whenever a new technique is being developed, the technique itself becomes such an over-riding consideration in the minds of those using it that the artistic qualities of the product are not given the importance that they deserve. It was so wonderful, in those days, that a drawing should move at all, that the pleasant design of the drawing and movement was apt to be neglected.

But we are able to take advantage of the great progress made in animation, and the greatly improved design of characters and settings in present-day cartoons. So we should be able to achieve attractive results, even if considerations of costs impose limitations on our technique.

It is, of course, only in black and white that this simplified method can be used. A colour film makes the use of cells absolutely essential, but it is unlikely that we will progress to colour until we have made several successful productions in black and white.

In any case, this experience in economy of scene design will be valuable when a more ambitious production is planned.

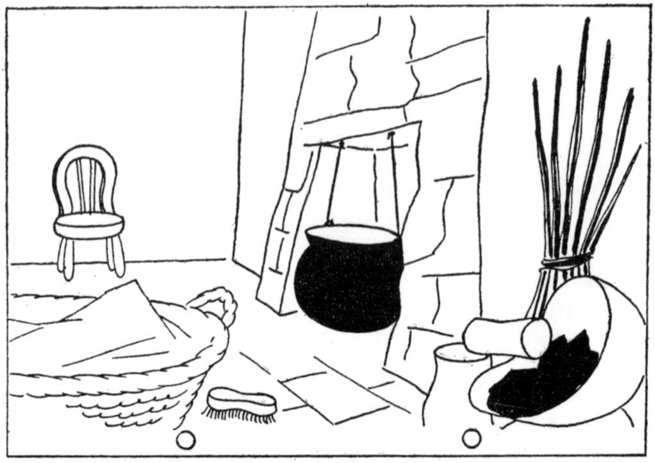

1

The components of one frame of a scene. (1) The background. (2) The first cell, registered to the basket on the background. (3) The second cell. A repeat animation, registered to the cauldron on the background. (4) The complete scene.

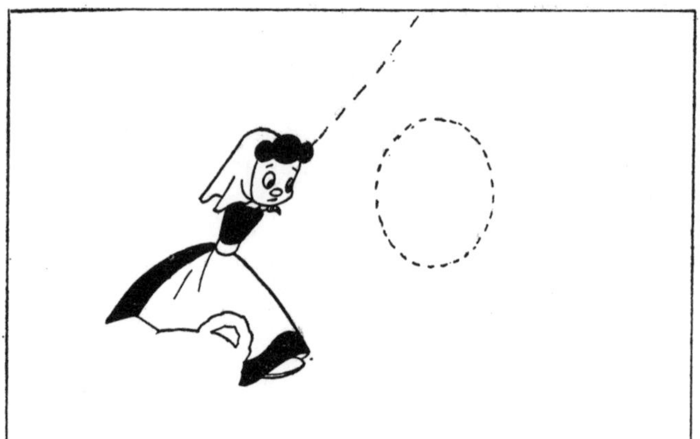

2

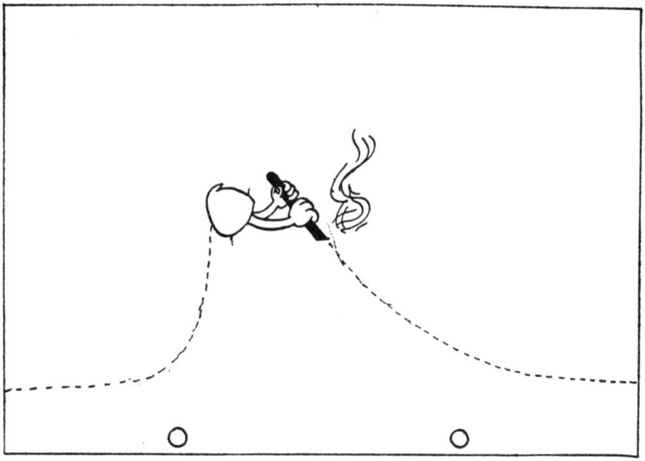

3

Dotted lines show the cut paper method. Smoke alone on bottom level. (2) Cut a hole, or half-way round the figure, to show smoke. (3) Cut all round, to fit over (2). (1) Background on cell. Lines crossing the figure omitted.

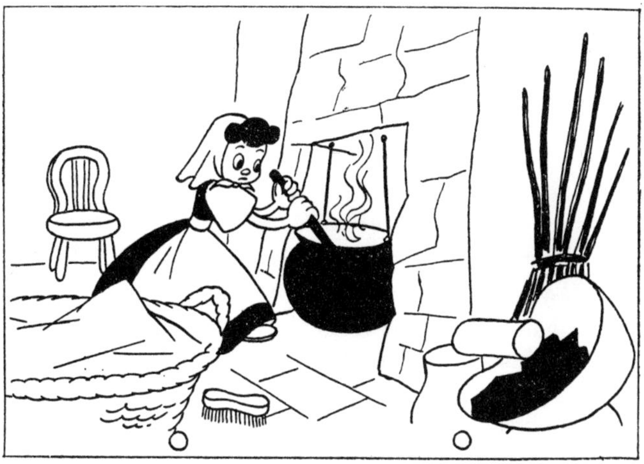

4

Simplifying Matters

If we decide to use the cut paper method, we shall have to modify the design of our scenes accordingly.

We must make the background as simple as possible, leaving the maximum amount of white space in the centre of the screen.

Cut out foregrounds, either on paper, or drawn on cell behind which the characters move, can be painted in full tone, and help to give depth to the scene.

Close ups can often be designed without using any background at all.

Plan figures and moving objects in black and white, and at the most, one tone of grey.

For the finished animation trace the drawings on a whiter and more opaque paper than the thin stuff used for the animation sketches.

In tracing, take very great care to maintain a uniform thickness of line in every drawing. If one part of a figure, such as the feet or legs, remain still while the rest is moving, every tracing of this part must be in exact register with the previous one, or it will jitter violently when the finished film is projected on the screen.

If one part remains still for any length of time, it is a great saving of labour to make only one tracing of this, cut it out and place it over the other drawings on which only the moving part appears.

When the outlines are completed, fill in the blacks with Indian ink or poster colour brushed on very dry, so that it does not distort and crinkle the paper. There must, of course, be an absolutely uniform black on every drawing.

Half Tones

Avoid half tones—grey tones between black and white—unless absolutely essential, as it is much more difficult to make them completely even.

With practice, this can be done with water colour or coloured ink. A colour is easier to put on evenly than grey.

Usually a light red reproduces well as a middle tone.

Start by mixing a sufficient quantity for the whole scene, and keep it well stirred. Brush it on quickly, using as few brush strokes as possible and being very sparing with colour. While it is wet, blot it quickly with clean blotting paper.

Better results will be obtained with small areas of tone than large ones.

If you make a mistake, don't attempt to go over the space again. It is better to scrap the whole drawing. But sometimes the space can be cut out, and the tone painted on another small piece of paper which is stuck on behind.

Finishing the Scenes

The next stage is to decide where the sheets of paper have to be cut to build up the complete scene. This presents some fascinating problems and is unrivalled as an exercise in ingenuity.

Probably the only solution to some particularly tricky problems is to trace a few drawings, or even one complete level of animation, on cell. In this case the colour that has been used for the half tone on the paper drawings will have to be accurately matched and used for filling in the cell. Often white paint will need darkening slightly with grey to make it match the white of the paper.

Poster colour to which gum has been added will adhere to cell long enough to be photographed if it is handled very carefully, but it is worth while to go to the trouble of painting in oil colour if very many cells are used.

In cutting paper drawings, don't make the fatal error of cutting off the peg holes. Cut each drawing in a slightly different place. Then, if the paper cuts do show slightly on the film, it will not be so obvious. But with care paper cuts can be completely invisible, if the lighting and exposure in photography are correct (p. 108).

An important point to remember is that the number of levels of cell used must remain the same throughout the whole scene. Although cell is transparent and colourless, each thickness used does cut down the amount of light reaching the camera. If we start a scene with only one cell above the white paper, and during the scene we add another, the whole scene will suddenly darken to quite an obvious extent.

To avoid this, use blank cells which are discarded when the animation on cell appears. This is another factor which has to be noted in the camera chart.

Making a Camera Chart

Even for the most simple scenes, consisting of only one level of animation, it is advisable to prepare a camera chart.

This consists of sheets of paper ruled with horizontal lines, each representing one frame of film as shown opposite.

Vertical columns represent the different levels of animation, the left-hand column being the lowest level. The numbers of the animation drawings are written downwards in the vertical columns, so that, by reading across horizontally, we have the numbers and the order of the drawings or cells which should be on the pegs together with any frame.

If there is a blank cell, the word "blank" is written in the appropriate column.

If a background pans along, the background itself is calibrated with the divisions it moves for each frame. The divisions are numbered, and the numbers written in the column headed "Background".

Another vertical column is headed "Camera", and in this the positions and lengths of mixes and fades are indicated, and also the frame by frame changes in the position of the camera if it is to track closer to or away from the field.

Although the example of a camera chart given may at first sight appear to be only a meaningless jumble of figures, charting ceases to be a headache for the animator after a little experience.

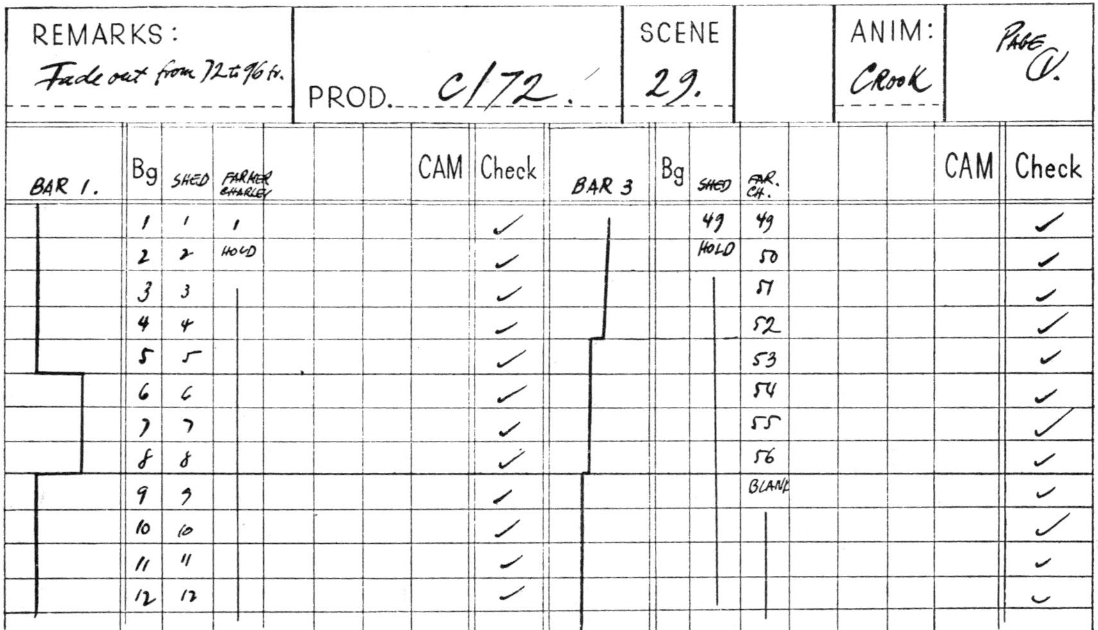

Camera chart, using two cell levels. No need for printed form—could be ruled by hand.

Using Colour

When you have become reasonably proficient at making black-and-white cartoons, you may like to try your hand at a production in colour.

From the point of view of animation there is nothing difficult about it; you prepare the individual drawings—this time on celluloid—in the same way as for black-and-white.

Then comes the big job: colouring. The two important points to watch in colouring are evenness of application, and uniformity of colour throughout the film.

In other words, evenly coloured areas must not be patchy, not even in just a few frames.

Further, the hue and depth of tone of the same colour must not change from one shot to another. This is a matter of continuity as much as anything; if our hero wears a scarlet cloak in one shot and a blood red one in the next, the effect will be as queer as if he had suddenly changed from long trousers to knickerbockers for no apparent reason.

So, use the same pigments throughout to make up any particular colour, and be specially careful about blending. Make the colour up in the right strength, and do not dilute concentrated colours to obtain different hues, or you will have great difficulty in matching them.

Photography

The camera and rostrum on which the final stage of the production of the film is carried out, can be as simple or as complicated as our ingenuity or our pockets can make it.

The set-up must, however, fulfil certain minimum requirements. As bad camera work or inferior equipment can easily ruin all the work we have put into the animation, it is worth while to spend time, trouble and money in making it as efficient as we possibly can.

What the Camera Must Do

1. We shall invariably photograph the drawings one by one. So the camera must be capable of exposing one frame at a time.

This is possible with most of the standard clockwork-operated cameras.

2. The camera must be capable of *focusing* on the field which is used for the animation. If it has a focusing lens there should be no difficulty about this.

The close distance at which the drawings are photographed is, however, usually too near for a fixed focus lens, especially as the *stop* used is likely to be a large one.

This difficulty can usually be solved by using a *supplementary lens* in front of the camera lens. If the camera lens is set to infinity, the supplementary lens should be of the same focal length as the distance between the camera lens and the drawings.

3. The camera should have a viewfinder which looks directly through the taking lens. If it has an indirect viewfinder, this will not be centred on the same point as the camera lens. With some finders this *parallax* error can be

adjusted to make the finder accurate for the close distances at which it will be used.

If the camera does not have a direct viewfinder, focusing will be a matter of trial and error. This is not of very great importance as once the focus is found, it need not be altered. Tracking shots, of course, will be out of the question.

4. The lens should be fitted with an adjustable *iris diaphragm*. This will allow us to vary the exposure to suit the lighting and also to produce fades. Again, nearly every camera has this feature.

So the camera which fulfils our minimum requirements is a simple affair. With it we shall be able to shoot our animation quite successfully, but certain effects will be beyond our reach.

We shall be able to fade out and to fade in, by closing down the iris from its normal stop, or opening it up to its normal stop in stages, and making an exposure at each stage.

But we shall be unable to mix or wipe, and we cannot obtain the many useful effects of double exposure, or superimposition.

For these the camera must also be capable of running backwards.

And if we want to be able to make tracking shots, the lens must have a focusing mount and a viewfinder which looks directly through the taking lens so that we can focus correctly in a number of different positions.

Further Refinements

Two more refinements will make it the perfect instrument, so far as any camera (pernickety creatures which most film cartoonists soon learn to distrust) can be considered perfect.

1. Registration pins fitted to the gate. These fit into one or more of the sprocket holes as the gate closes, locking the film into position while the exposure is made.

This ensures a steady picture. Moreover, we can make several exposures on each frame, and be sure that the image on the film each time will be in exact register with all the others, as the film is always held into exactly the same position. Fitting such registration pins, of course, is a skilled engineering job, and adds considerably to the cost of the camera.

2. A set of interchangeable lenses, of different focal lengths. With these, we can take close-ups, medium shots and long shots without altering the position of the camera. Also, our tracking range becomes much greater.

The Stand for the Camera

Let's leave the camera on one side for the moment and consider the *rostrum*.

That is the frame on which the camera and the board which holds the animation drawings are mounted. The most important point about it is that it must be rigid.

It can be made of wood, with four stout uprights kept the correct distance apart by battens at top and bottom, and as much cross bracing as is necessary.

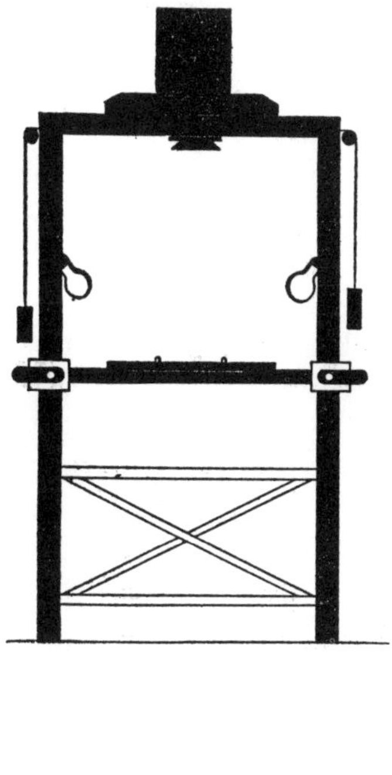

It should be as high as possible, according to the height of the room in which it is going to be used. The back and feet are best firmly fixed to the wall and floor.

The floor of the room in which the rostrum is erected should be solid, without loose boards, and if possible, away from heavy traffic outside the house. If the floor vibrates while shooting is going on, we cannot expect a steady picture.

The camera and operating gear is fixed to a board, with a hole cut for the lens, at the top of the framework.

If the camera is going to track, holes are drilled at the corners of this board, and four metal collars, with setscrews, fixed above them. Four metal rods pass through these collars, and are fixed by brackets at top and bottom, to the uprights. The camera board will then slide up and down along these rods, and the setscrews will lock it in any position.

A length of wire cable is attached to each corner of the camera board, with a pulley above it on the top of the framework. The cables are passed over the pulleys, and counterweights are fixed to the ends. The weights are adjusted until the board can be moved up and down easily by hand, but will remain stationary if left alone.

The guide rods for the camera board also pass through the corners of the easel, and through battens screwed to it at each side. These battens are fastened to the four uprights by G-clamps when the correct position for the easel has been found.

This position should be at a convenient working height which allows sufficient distance from the camera to cover the standard field.

The Animation Board

This is another flat piece of board. A small drawing-board is very suitable, about four times the area of the field.

On this are fixed a pair of registration pegs just as they were on the light box.

On a sheet of animation paper draw a series of horizontal and vertical lines, parallel and at right angles to the pegs. Place the frame mask over it, on the pegs. Then adjust the animation board and the camera so that the lens will cover the area within the frame mask, and the vertical and horizontal lines are parallel to the edges of the viewfinder.

To achieve this the easel must be adjusted at right angles to the centre line of the camera lens. When this position is found, the animation board holding the pegs can be screwed down to the easel.

However, it is not advisable to fix it permanently until a few test frames have been taken and developed to test the accuracy of its position. This is best left until focus and exposure tests are made.

The Pressure Plate

When a scene is photographed, the various layers of paper and cell which make up the complete picture must be kept quite flat. Otherwise the paper cuts and the objects on cell will throw shadows, and the small creases in the cells will reflect light into the lens, causing halation.

They are, therefore, pressed firmly down under a sheet of plate glass, which is held firmly in a wooden or metal frame.

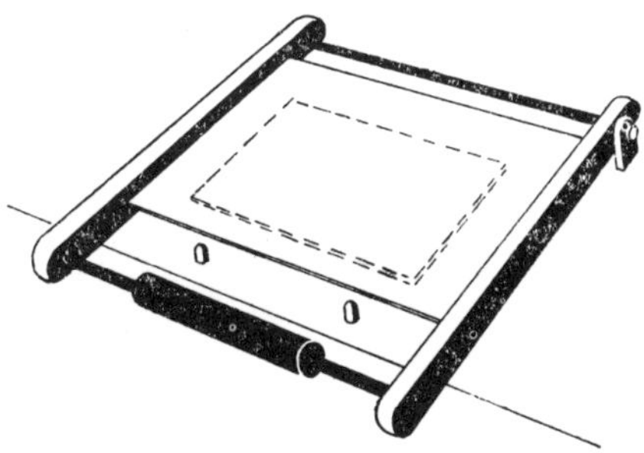

The frame is fixed to the animation board by stout hinges at the top of the field, and, of course, well outside it.

A thin sheet of sponge rubber, felt, or even a pad of blotting paper is laid down over the area of the field to make a resilient surface for the cells and paper to be pressed down upon.

As considerable pressure will have to be put on this frame during each exposure, it should be very solid in construction. The sheet of glass should be quite thick, ordinary window glass is definitely not good enough. It must also be completely unmarked and without flaws, or these will appear on each frame of our film; a most undesirable trademark.

It will save time in photography if a spring or counterweight is fixed to the frame so that it will swing up as soon as pressure is released, to allow the drawings to be changed.

Uniform Lighting

The next problem to be tackled is the lighting.

The lights are best fixed to the animation board. Then if the position of the board is changed the distance between the lights and the field will not vary, and the exposure will remain constant.

The simplest, and often the best, method is to arrange a batten of four lamps on each side of the field with a simple reflector made of tin-plate.

The power of the lamps can then be varied to suit the maximum aperture of the lens, the exposure time of the camera and the aperture of the shutter (all of which control the amount of light reaching the film).

The lighting must be even over the whole field. If it drops off anywhere, or causes a *hot spot* because light is reflected into the lens from the glass surface, there will be dark or light patches on the screen when the film is projected.

The angle of light is, therefore, important.

You get reflections if the lamps are too close to the camera. Let them shine on the cell surface at a wide angle instead, so that any reflected light is well clear of the camera lens.

Evenness of lighting is best tested by a photo-electric brightness meter or exposure meter. Run the meter slowly over the whole field, and keep adjusting the position and angle of the lights until it shows the same reading in every position.

If a meter is not available, try to trace changes in the intensity of the light by scanning the field, with a sheet of white paper on the pegs, and the frame mask in place, through a dark filter.

This is not a reliable method, though, so in any case a test should be made by photographing the lighted field of view on a strip of film in the camera. Have this processed and run it through the projector (preferably joined end to end in a continuous loop) and you will soon notice any unevenness in lighting.

This is also the best way of making sure that no light from the surface of the cells or the glass is reflected into the lens.

Two small floodlights, each of 250 watts, fixed to brackets on each side of the field will probably be found to be more efficient and more easily adjusted than the simple batten, but the trouble with these is that they are apt to concentrate heat as well as light. If the lighting is too hot, cells will crinkle, patches of moisture will appear on them which are very difficult to get rid of, and photography will be a generally uncomfortable business.

When the lighting has been rigged up, go on a search for unwanted reflections. Paint everything on the rostrum matt black, including the underside of the lens mount. It is a complete waste of film to take beautiful pictures of the lens, reflected in the glass, but it is surprising how often this is done! Reflections have a habit of occurring from the most unlikely places, so hood the lens to protect it from rays as much as possible.

The Film to Use

You will probably shoot most of your cartoons on *reversal film*. This is the cheapest and simplest way for amateur use.

When you send the exposed film back for processing, it is directly developed and reversed into a positive; so the strip of film you project is actually the same as the one you exposed. The processing charge is included in the price when you buy the film.

There are several makes and types of reversal film available in the three substandard sizes.

The best choice is a *slower* (less sensitive) film stock rather than one of the fast types. The reason for this is that cartoon drawings should reproduce fairly contrasty, and slower films generally give more contrast.

Suitable films are *Gevaert* Micropan and Superpan, *Kodak* Plus X and possibly Super X, and *Pathe* S.X. Pan.

These films will need more exposure than high speed types, but that does not matter greatly, as we have lighting and exposure conditions completely under our control.

Alternatively, if we want more than one copy of the film, we can use *negative* stock. This is processed to a negative only, and has to be printed again onto positive film to produce the finished film for projection. We can in this way get as many copies of our original film as we want. Naturally filming becomes more expensive in this way—the cost of sensitive material is doubled—but we have much more control over exposure as well as the contrast of the final copy.

Suitable types are *Gevaert* Gevapan 27 *Ilford* Pan F, and *Kodak* Plus X.

As we can ask the processing laboratory to increase the contrast when making the positive print, we can use even high speed stock such as *Ilford* H.P.3 or *Kodak* Tri X for photographing the drawings.

If we use the cut paper method of animation and make our drawings without any half tones, high contrast becomes even more important.

In that case the best choice is to photograph the drawings on *positive* stock. This is a slow but very contrasty film used for making prints from negative film. If we use it in the camera, we shall, of course, obtain a negative. This has to be printed on another positive film to give the final projection copy.

As the film is so slow, we shall need more light or a larger stop.

On the other hand, it will not reproduce half tones easily. This means that the paper cuts will show much less (if at all) than with a film that reproduces subtle changes of tone. As we cannot use a range of tones in any case with the paper cutting method, this is no disadvantage.

We can also use colour film for photographing coloured drawings.

The films to use are *Anscochrome* (8 and 16 mm.) or *Kodachrome* (8 and 16 mm.). In either case we shall need the artificial light type, so as to obtain the best colour rendering. Both *Anscochrome Tungsten* film and *Kodachrome Type A* film are balanced for Photofloods.

With any other light source we shall need suitable colour correction filters in front of the camera lens. These are obtainable from the makers.

When shooting in colour, watch the following points.

Make sure the voltage of your electric mains which feeds the lamps is constant. Variations in voltage will affect the colour of the light sufficiently to change the colour balance of the final film. This will be very noticeable when the film is projected on the screen.

Shoot the whole film on one batch of colour stock. Different batches vary slightly in colour balance, which again may be annoying when the finished film is assembled.

For the same reason send all the film to be processed together.

So first choose the film, and load the camera with it. This is not an unnecessary hint. More than once a whole scene has been shot with no film in the camera! And if you *do* remember to load, don't forget to take the lens cap off!

Before starting to shoot, make a routine check of the camera. Always check the items in the same order and it will soon become a habit.

Making Tests

We are now ready to start on a further series of tests, for exposure and focus.

Don't be too anxious to start shooting animation before making exhaustive tests, as it will almost certainly prove to be wasted material, time and effort.

For each of these tests we shall need to prepare a separate test card to be put on the pegs and photographed. They can, of course, be shot at one time, and sent for processing together, but we will consider them separately.

About ten seconds of film will be needed for each test, so that they can be projected in a continuous loop. Studying them in the hand is likely to lead to deceptive conclusions.

How to Expose

As we have to photograph the drawings one by one, a camera with a single frame mechanism is almost essential.

A camera can expose a single frame of film at a time in several ways.

Most generally used is the clockwork mechanism which can be set to make a single exposure every time the button is pressed. The only point to remember here is to keep the spring fully wound, or the exposure time will gradually increase as the motor runs slower.

Some of the cheaper cine cameras do not have a single-frame speed at all. Single exposures are then a question of tapping the exposure button with just the right amount of force to make one exposure. Needless to say, this is a highly unsatisfactory procedure, and such cameras are not really suitable for filming cartoons.

The hand-turned camera is only suitable for black and white drawings without half tones. Photographed on a slow contrasty film, it is virtually impossible to ensure that each exposure is exactly the same, however careful we are. This means that successive frames will be slightly under- or over-exposed. The half tones will vary in density and flicker when projected. Even with plain black and white we must take care to turn the handle each time at the same speed. Practise doing this, with a regular sweeping movement of the arm, counting "one-two-three" while turning the handle, and stop each time in the same position.

An electrically operated camera is best. The simplest form is a solenoid which operates the trigger magnetically when we press a button.

Most cameras in professional studios are equipped with an electric motor, which runs all the time the camera is being used, at a constant speed. It drives the camera by means of a clutch, which is thrown into gear when the exposure is made, and automatically disengages after one revolution.

Controlling Exposure

In all cameras the exposure is variable in two ways:

(*a*) By adjusting the amount of light which reaches the film. This is done by the adjustable iris fitted to the lens, which increases or reduces the diameter of the aperture or *stop* through which the light passes.

(*b*) By varying the time during which the film is exposed to light. Most cine cameras expose the film by means of a shutter which rotates between the lens and the camera gate. The shutter has a segment cut out of it, which allows light to pass through to the film once for every turn of the shutter. We can increase or decrease this segment to increase or cut down exposure time. If the shutter is not fitted as an adjustable one, leave any adjustments to an expert. In motor-driven cameras, adjusting the speed of the motor has, within limits, the same effect as adjusting the shutter aperture.

Making an Exposure Test

Prepare an exposure test card, the same size as a normal animation drawing. Divide this into six areas of grey, ranging from off-white to very dark. Two thick lines, one black, one white, should cross each area.

Place the card on the pegs beneath the camera, and

photograph it for twelve individual frames at each lens stop; each group of frames being separated by a few frames of a label stating the stop used.

If you are using colour film, include a colour chart of squares of blue-green, green, yellow orange, and red with the test chart you are filming.

If desired, the test can be repeated with different total wattage of lamps, the power and number of lamps also being stated on the labels.

Send the reel to be processed. When you get it back, examine a frame in each group with a magnifying lens and also run the whole reel through a projector.

Note the contrast between the white line and the lightest greys, and the black line and the darkest greys.

If the off-white and the white merge together, the film is *over-exposed.* If the darkest grey and the black merge together, it is *under-exposed.*

If the print shows darker or lighter patches anywhere in the field, which were not on the original card, the lighting is uneven.

If the result is under-exposed with the largest stop and the brightest light, you must use a faster film; or, if this is not practicable, widen the shutter aperture.

If it is over-exposed at the smallest stop and the dimmest light, use a slower film, decrease the shutter aperture, or fit a neutral density filter in front of the lens.

When choosing the lens aperture, which will be used as a standard exposure, remember that it may be necessary to increase or decrease the exposure for certain effects, so arrange to have at least one stop in hand either way.

When the best exposure has been chosen, set up a complete frame of a scene, and make another test for even lighting, and visible paper cuts.

If the lighting has been well balanced, and the glass is given even pressure, shadows will be reduced to a minimum, and the paper edges should be quite invisible. But it may be found that slightly adjusting the stop either way will help.

Accurate Focusing

Next comes the focusing test.

The subject put under the glass to focus on should contain the finest and closest lines possible.

A page of very small type will do. A pound note is better, if the exchequer can run to it. Best of all is a focusing wedge.

This can be purchased, or made in the following way. On a large sheet of white paper draw a number of fine black lines, close together, converging on a point. Across these draw other lines. Photograph this drawing on a miniature ($1 \times 1\frac{1}{2}$ ins.) size negative, and make a contact print. Mount the print on white card, and punch it for the pegs.

To start with, set the camera to the approximate distance needed for the lens and size of drawings.

If the camera has no direct view finder, the first trial focusing point will have to be estimated by the calibrations of distance on the lens mount. Stick a small piece of adhesive tape on the lens mount, and mark on it the chosen position. On each side of it make four more marks, close together. Number the middle mark 0 and the others +1, +2, +3 and +4 in one direction, and -1, -2, -3 and -4 in the other.

Expose a few frames at each of these points, labelling each group with the corresponding number. Examine the negative with a magnifying glass, and choose the point which gives the sharpest image. This point is then marked permanently on the lens mount.

Even if the camera has a view finder which enables it to be focused visually, it is worth while to make a test in this way, as pin point sharpness is very important in cartoon films. Also, as we are shooting at short distances and usually at a large stop, we have no great *depth of field.*

When these tests have been completed satisfactorily, we will be able to shoot straightforward animation.

However, more tests must be made if fades, mixes, wipes, or double exposure are required. The process for each of these is as follows:

Fades

These can be done either with the help of the iris diaphragm, by opening or shutting it in stages, a frame or two frames being exposed at each stage; or by wiring a dimmer into the lighting circuit.

The slide of the dimmer is calibrated. To fade out, the lights are dimmed from normal power until no image is recorded on the film. To fade in, they are brought back from this position to normal.

For fades with the iris diaphragm, the stop for normal exposure should be as large as possible, so that we have the greatest possible movement in which to calibrate the fade, from open to shut.

An extension arm should be fitted to the iris which swings round in an arc when the iris is moved. Cut a piece of card in the shape of this arc, and fix it so that the pointer slides along it. Mark on the card the normal open, and the fully closed positions. If the iris does not completely close, the last exposure of the fade out, or the first of the fade in, a completely black frame, will have to be made with the lens covered. Divide the scale between these two marks into 24, the most convenient number of frames for a fade. The calibrations will not be evenly spaced. For fading out, it will be found that the iris needs to close very slowly at first, speeding up at the middle and closing rapidly in the last few frames. The correct calibrations, which will give a smoothly and progressively darkening fade, can only be found by a series of tests. For fading in, use the same calibrations in the reverse order.

3' FADE IRIS

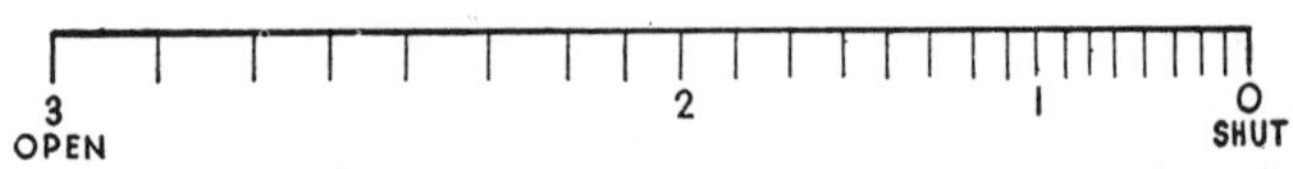

The dimmer has the advantage of making a fade possible at any lens stop. The calibrations are made in the same way, and will be in very much the same spacing as with the iris.

Longer or shorter fades can be made in various ways; taking two exposures at each position; putting the pointer between the calibrations; or missing out every other one, or two.

However, with colour film our dimmer is not much good, as the colour of the light changes as the lamps are dimmed. So in that case you will have to rely on the iris diaphragm.

Mixes

A mix is made by fading out on one scene, winding the film back so that the first frame of the fade out is again in the camera gate, then, shooting forwards again, fading in on the next scene. Like the fade it can be done with the iris diaphragm, or by a dimmer. The calibrations are made in the same way.

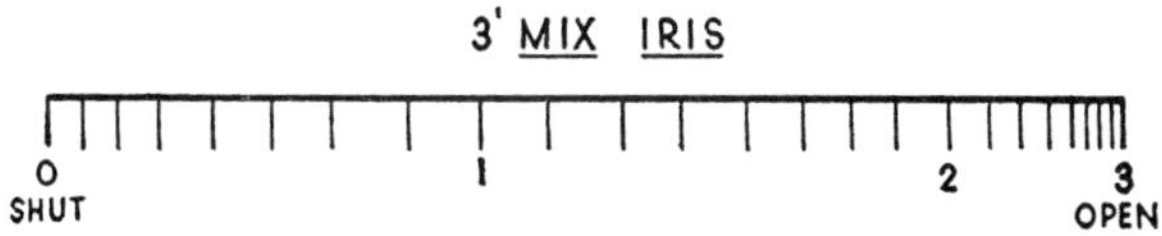

But the calibrations for a mix will be spaced differently to those for a fade. Each frame receives two exposures, one when fading out, and another when fading in, and these two fractional exposures must be made to total a full, normal exposure. If this is not done correctly, the film will be under- or over-exposed during the mix, and the screen will become lighter or darker.

For a mix, in fading in, the iris or dimmer will need to open slowly, speed up, and then slow down slightly again. The same calibrations are used in reverse. Again, testing is the only way to find the right answer.

In winding back between the two scenes, don't forget to cover the lens!

Wipes

As a simple example, take a wipe which has the form of a vertical line moving across the screen in 12 frames.

This line is animated to move across in the usual way, and it is traced on to cell *twice*.

One of these series of cells is numbered 1 to 12, and the other 1a to 12a. One series is filled in with black on the left-hand side of the line, between the line and the edge of the screen.

The other series is filled in in the same way, on the right-hand side of the line. If cells 1 and 1a are put on the pegs together, the screen will be completely black, and so on with all corresponding numbers.

We now wish to wipe from one scene to another. Over the first scene we put, in succession, cells 1 to 12, making one exposure on each. We then wind back 12 frames, and change the scene, putting cell 1a on the pegs over the scene. The part of the second scene which is uncovered by the wipe will be photographed on the part that was covered in the first scene. Shooting forwards, we now expose 12 frames with cells 1a to 12a in succession on the pegs.

Other forms of wipe are done in exactly the same way.

Tracking

Here the camera approaches, or moves away from, the field, one frame being exposed at each stage of the movement.

Before a tracking shot is photographed, the distance to be tracked is marked on a scale, and divided into the number of moves to be made. As the camera moves, a pointer moves along this scale.

At various points on the scale the focus must be altered to keep the image sharp all the way through. Check all these focusing points beforehand, and mark the lens mount with numbers corresponding to points on the scale where the focus is changed.

The camera must be held rigid at each stage while the exposure is made.

Fast tracks are very much easier than slow ones, as slight deviations from a straight line in the movement of the camera which are very difficult to avoid with any but the finest precision built equipment, are not so noticeable with faster movement.

A mix while tracking is very effective, and much less exacting than a straightforward tracking shot.

Double Exposure

Very interesting effects can be obtained by making two or more exposures on each frame of a scene, in the same way as we get interesting effects when we forget to wind on the film in our snapshot camera.

Animation of things such as smoke or clouds, which need to be nebulous and transparent, is traced on to black paper, and filled in in white or grey. The darker the grey, the more transparent the image will be.

After the main animation of the scene with the background has been shot, the film is wound back, and the animated clouds photographed. Even where the cloud, or whatever it is, does not appear until halfway through the scene, the film must always be wound back to the beginning of the scene, and plain black paper photographed. If this is not done, the part that has two exposures will appear lighter all over than the rest.

We can never double expose in this way to obtain a tone *darker* than the background. We can only add to the exposure, not subtract from it.

To obtain a transparent dark tone, such as shadows, the animation of the shadows is traced on a separate series of cells. These shadows are filled in solid black. Then the scene is photographed all through, without the shadows, at an exposure of about one stop less than normal. The film is wound back to the beginning of the scene, and the animation is repeated, this time with the addition of the shadows. The exposure should again be about one stop less than normal.

The result is transparent shadows. The degree of transparency can be varied by adjusting the two exposures, less exposure on the shadows making them more transparent. But the two part exposures must always add up to one full one. The correct balance of exposure should be determined by making tests before starting the scene.

This trick can only be done if the camera gate is fitted with register pins, as the two exposures must exactly coincide on the film, or a double image will result.

Just a Few More Aids

The cameraman is not only responsible for the quality of the photography, but also for the manipulation of moving backgrounds and the changing of animation drawings and cells. His work demands very great concentration.

If the photography can be made a two-men job, the time taken will be more than halved.

Any devices which make his work easier will result in films of better quality. A frame counter on the camera, for instance, will save him headaches in complicated scenes.

Sliding wooden strips, fitted into grooves in the animation board on which panning backgrounds can be pinned, reduce the amount of care and trouble to be taken in ensuring that these movements are smooth.

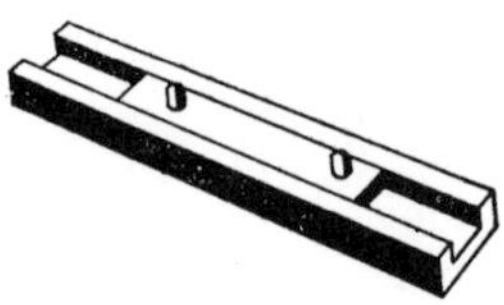

Tables fitted with nests of shelves will help him to keep animation drawings sorted out in their correct order, and save endless trouble, particularly with complicated repeats.

Thought, time and money expended on the camera and rostrum and its equipment will be amply repaid. After all, the cameraman's work is the only part of all the work put into a film that the audience actually sees!

INDEXED GLOSSARY

ACTION. Movement of characters and objects in order to tell the story 76

ACTION SKETCH. Rough drawing indicating a stage, or series of stages, of an action 93

ANGLE. (a) The assumed viewpoint of the observer (i.e. an imaginary camera) which determines the perspective in laying out a scene. For variety in continuity a different angle is often used in long shots, medium shots and close-ups of the same subject 78

(b) Of lens. The angle at which the outermost rays of light passing through the lens meet at the focal point 17

ANIMATION. The art of giving apparent movement to inanimate objects. The word is also used for the sequence of drawings made to create the movement, and for the movement itself when seen on the screen 10

ANIMATION BOARD. Adjustable board on the camera rostrum on which the pressure pad, register pegs, panning slides and glass frame are fitted 106

APERTURE. The size of the opening in the iris or shutter of the camera, controlling the amount of light reaching the film 113

BACKGROUND. (a) The setting against which action takes place. It may be drawn or painted on paper, with the animation cells placed over it, or drawn on cell, and placed over animation paper ... 85

(b) Objects or characters appearing far away from the observer

(c) Action or sound subsidiary to the main action or sound ... 64

BACKWARD TAKE. Photographing a scene with the camera running in reverse. Frequently used to make a line grow (or "run out") from a point. The line is painted on cell and part of it scraped off for each exposure. When the film is projected forwards, the line will appear to grow. Footprints, trails from aircraft and many other effects can easily be obtained by this method 104

BLANK. Cell without a drawing used in photography to keep the number of cell levels constant throughout a scene, to avoid changes of tone 99

BUMP IN OR OUT. Causing an object to appear or disappear in one frame of film. A very economical, but often interesting effect, especially if accompanied by a sound.

CALIBRATIONS. Marks to indicate the movement of a background in panning shots, the movement of the camera in tracks, or on a line as a guide to the position of in-between drawings 85

CELLS. Transparent sheets on which animation drawings are traced. Short for celluloid, but this material is not recommended, as it is highly inflammable. Cellulose acetate, or other colourless plastic is usually used 12, 92

CELL FLASH. Bright patch on film caused by reflection of light from uneven surface of cell into the lens 108

CELL LEVELS. The layers of cell, each bearing an animation drawing, which are placed on the pegs over the background to build up a complete frame. Advisable not to use more than three. Number must remain constant throughout scene (see "Blank")... ... 93

CHARACTER. Representation of a personality, as distinct from an object (*q.v.*) 73

CHARACTER SKETCHES. Drawings defining features, proportions, clothes, etc., of a character, and specifying his type expressions, and reactions 75

CHARTS. Camera: Frame by frame instructions to cameraman as to cell levels, background movement, etc. 100

Music/Speech: Frame by frame analysis of sound track, so that animation will synchronise with it 91

CLEAN-UP. Making finished drawings from roughs (*q.v.*). Removing surplus ink, paint, finger-prints and dust from cells before photography. A very important procedure.

COLOUR KEY. A specimen cell of each character or object painted in colours or tones as a guide to the painting of the whole scene. Designed together with the background 92

CONCERTINA MOVEMENT. Movement transferred from one character or object, or one of their parts, to another... 56

CONTINUITY. The smooth unfolding of the story of a film, by means of progressive changes of scene 77

CUT. (a) Direct change of scene in successive frames 79

(b) Removal of frames from the film.

CUT-BACK. Correction of a mistake in photography. A label is photographed stating the number of frames on which the mistake occurs (cut back X frames) and these frames are shot again. The mistake is then cut out of the print before projection.

CUT-OUTS. (a) Things which do not change in outline during movement can be animated by hand as a cut-out drawing. A guide showing the portion of the cut-out for each frame is drawn on cell, and placed on the pegs. The cut-out is put in position, under the guide. The guide is removed and the exposure made. Simple animation can be made with jointed figures in this way 94

(b) The foreground of a scene which goes over the animation can be drawn on paper and cut out to save an additional cell level ... 98

CUTTING COPY. The complete film made up of separate scenes joined together. It is not usually possible to photograph the film straight through from beginning to end, with all scenes in the correct order. After final adjustments are made to the cutting copy, the negatives are cut and assembled to match it, and a print made without joins 12

DIRECTOR. The person who takes responsibility for what appears on the screen and the methods by which the result is achieved ... 13

DOUBLE FRAME. One animation drawing photographed for two frames instead of one. Either halves the speed of a movement or the number of drawings required for an action of a certain time. Triple and quadruple frame animation is possible for very slow movement. Is more likely to cause optical jitter (*q.v.*) than single frame ... 31

EFFECTS. Sound: Sounds accompanying movements to increase their realism. Not necessarily the natural sound 81
Animation: Reproduction of natural effects, such as rain, fire, water, in animation 119

FADE-IN. The scene gradually appears from black ... 79, 116

FADE-OUT. The scene gradually darkens to black ... 79, 116

FIELD. The area which a lens will reproduce as an image on the film 17

FOCAL LENGTH. The distance from the optical centre of a lens to the point at which rays of light passing through it converge. (The focal point) 17

FRAME. (a) One picture on the film 14

(b) The background, cell levels, cut-outs and foreground which are assembled on the pegs under the camera to be photographed so that they will appear on a frame of film 107

FRAME GLASS. Sheet of glass used to press down upon the cells under the camera to keep them flat 107

FRAME MASK. Space within which scenes and movement are designed. Its dimensions are the same as the field covered by the lens at a given distance. Registered to the pegs in the same way as animation drawings 20

GATE. Apparatus in camera and projector to hold each frame momentarily still behind the lens 14

GUIDE-LINES. See "Calibrations, Cut-Outs".

HOLD. Photograph one drawing on several frames, so that it appears still on the screen 101

HOT-SPOT. Part of the field which is over-illuminated. Appears as an over-exposed patch on the film 108

IN-BETWEENS. Drawings between two key positions (*q.v.*) ... 29

INERTIA. Tendency of a body to preserve its state of rest, or motion in a straight line, until that state is changed by external force ... 48

IRIS. A circular opening, which can be made to expand or contract:
(a) in the lens, to control exposure 104
(b) over-animation, to change the scene 80

JITTER. Uncontrolled movement on the screen caused by faulty animation, tracing or camera work 98

JITTER, OPTICAL. Flicker on the screen caused by animation which is not sympathetic to the eye. Objects in strong tonal contrast with the background, whose shape does not harmonise with the line of movement are the worst offenders. Their successive images are retained by the eye longer than normal, which causes an apparent double image 34

KEYS. Animation drawing of the principal positions in a movement. Keys are made of positions where any part of the figure stops, starts, or changes direction 29

LAYOUT. Design of a scene, including background, characters in correct relative size, colours cell levels and camera movement... 11

LIGHT BOX. Animation desk with registration pegs and glass drawing surface illuminated from below 15

LINE TEST. Sequence of pencil animation drawings photographed and projected, usually in negative, to check quality of animation before proceeding with tracing on to cells 32, 93

MIX. One scene fades out, at the same time as another is fading in, so that the two scenes are superimposed for a short period 79, 117

MOMENTUM. The amount of motion in a body. The product of its mass and velocity. Used loosely to describe the tendency of a moving body to remain moving (see "Inertia") 48

MULTIPLANE. Elaboration of camera rostrum. The animation board has a plate-glass base, in place of the pressure pad and a number of glass sheets are placed beneath it, at varying distances, each carrying animation or background on cell. They are lit and operated independently, and enable many different planes of perspective to be photographed at once, giving an illusion of a third dimension.

OBJECT. Thing which does not normally move of its own volition, but can be made to do so in animation.

OPTICAL AXIS. Line passing through the optical centre and the focal point of a lens 17

OPTICAL CENTRE. Point in centre of lens which a ray of light will pass through without being deviated.

OPTICALS. Mixes, Fades, Wipes, etc., made by the processing laboratories on an optical printing machine after the scenes have been photographed instead of in the camera during photography. Entails making duplicate negatives.

PAN. Contraction of *panorama*. In live action, the camera pivots and sweeps round an arc for an horizontal pan, and tilts up or down for a vertical pan. This effect is reproduced in animation by a background sliding past the camera 79

PANNING GEAR. Wooden strips sliding in grooves on the animation board to which pan backgrounds are attached, to prevent uncontrolled movement 120

PARALLAX. The difference between the image seen through the viewfinder and the image recorded by the lens, due to the lens and viewfinder being in different positions. Increases as the subject is brought nearer to the camera. Can be remedied to a certain extent by tilting the viewfinder, so that its axis and the optical axis of the lens coincide at the position of the subject 103

PRESSURE PLATE/PAD. A device to enable background and cells to be photographed flat at even overall pressure. It consists of a sheet of plate-glass in a wood or metal frame hinged to the animation board. Beneath it is a pad of felt or several thicknesses of cloth, blotting paper, or sponge rubber 107

PUNCH. Used to punch holes in animation paper and cells for the purpose of registration (*q.v.*) 16

REFLECTIONS. Parts of the rostrum, the camera, or their surroundings reflected in the glass and photographed. Can be avoided by carefully painting all parts with matt black and shielding the lens and the lights. Are more troublesome with darker backgrounds and larger fields 108

REGISTRATION. To ensure correct position of animated drawings and cells, in relation to one another, background and camera ... 14

REGISTER HOLES. Holes punched in animation paper and cell corresponding to register pegs 15

REGISTER PEGS. A metal bar fitted with pegs designed to keep animation in correct register 16

REGISTER PINS. Device in camera gate to ensure that each frame of film is in exactly the same position as preceding and following frames 104

RE-TAKE. Shooting a scene again, owing to unsatisfactory result the first time.

ROSTRUM. Rigid support for the camera and the animation board, so that they do not alter position relative to each other in an uncontrolled way 105

ROSTRUM CAMERA. Apparatus for producing an image on cine-film. Its minimum requirements for animation work are that it must be capable of exposing one frame of film at a time as required ... 105

ROSTRUM CAMERAMAN. The operator of the camera. His duties, apart from photography, usually include changing cells, animating cut-outs by hand and operating the rostrum 120

ROSTRUM CAMERA REPORT. A detailed description of a scene, its footage, stock used, processing required, etc., which may accompany the exposed film to the laboratory.

RUN OUT. In animation: Cause a line or shape to grow or from a point

In photography: Exhaust the supply of film in the magazine. This usually occurs in the middle of a scene and means re-taking, so it is advisable to keep an accurate record of all film used from a roll 111

SCRIPTS. (a) Illustrated: The rough idea of the story, with "thumbnail" sketches 11, 76

(b) Timed, or Shooting: A detailed specification, showing the time of each action, divided into scenes 81

SET-UP. Term used for the field covered by the camera at a given distance from the drawings on the animation board 17

SET-UP KEY. A controlling drawing to indicate the position of one or more set-ups for the guidance of the rostrum cameraman.

SEQUENCE. Any number of consecutive scenes which together express a situation.

SHOOTING. Photography.

SHOT. A scene.

SINGLE FRAME. Each animation drawing photographed for one frame only 31

SPROCKET HOLES. The holes on cine film by which the film is guided through the camera, and held still in the gate. Of exactly the same dimensions, and an equal distance apart. On the edges of 35 mm., 16 mm. and 8 mm. film, between the frames in the centre on 9.5 film 14

SQUASH. Distortion of animated forms 50

STOP. Size of the aperture in the iris controlling the amount of light reaching the film 104

STORY BOARD. Board to display the action and layout sketches of an animated film, in sequence 70

SYMPATHETIC MOVEMENT (see "Jitter-Optical"). Movement on the screen which the eye will readily accept as continuous 34

SYNCHRONISATION. (a) Animating so that an action will occur at the same time as its accompanying sound... 91

(b) Matching the cutting copy to the sound track so that a married print can be made with sound on the same film as the picture.

TAKE. The photography of a scene. Each new take of the same scene is numbered (T.1, T.2, etc.).

TAKE-BOARD. Label photographed at the start of each scene, for identification purposes. States the title of film, number of scene and number of take.

TEST CAMERA. Camera and rostrum usually of a simple type used solely for line testing (*q.v.*).

TESTING. Avoiding subsequent headaches by making sure of exposure, lighting, focus, before shooting begins 112

TIMING. Determining speed of action and sound 22

TURNTABLE. Apparatus on the animation board which enables the field to rotate through 360 degrees, securable in any position. Used for panning backgrounds diagonally.

TREATMENT. Preliminary to writing script. Marshalling of ideas and situations suitable for the film in hand.

TRIP GEAR. Apparatus used in photography which enables single frames of film, or a succession of single frames, to be exposed at constant speed, by means of a clutch, and an electric motor ... 113

THREE-TO-ONE GEAR. Apparatus used in photography in Technicolor by the successive frame method. Enables three exposures to be made at a time by one operation of the trip gear (see). Each exposure is through a different coloured filter.

WIPE. One scene appears to slide over the preceding scene. The dividing line between the scenes can take any desired form ... 117

FOCAL BOOKS ON CINEMATOGRAPHY

THE TECHNIQUE OF THE FILM CUTTING ROOM

By Ernest Walter

Details the functions of the editor in relation to each stage in the production of a large scale film.

2nd ed., 316 pp., 167 illus.

THE TECHNIQUE OF FILM EDITING

Compiled by Karel Reisz and Gavin Millar

The British Film Academy appointed ten outstanding film editors to summarize their views and experience.

2nd ed., 412 pp., 346 illus., casebound and paperback.

THE TECHNIQUE OF FILM MUSIC

By John Huntley and Roger Manvell

Illustrated by extracts from important films, it covers documentary, experimental and cartoon productions.

2nd ed., 312 pp., 176 illus.

THE TECHNIQUE OF EDITING 16 mm FILMS

By John Burder

Starts with basic matters of film gauge, equipment and editing facilities and goes on to discuss the pure mechanics of editing.

3rd ed., 152 pp., 169 illus.

THE TECHNIQUE OF SPECIAL EFFECTS CINEMATOGRAPHY

By Raymond Fielding

Describes every special effects technique in use throughout the world.

3rd ed., 426 pp., 505 illus.

THE TECHNIQUE OF THE SOUND STUDIO

By Alec Nisbett

This book is for anyone concerned with putting radio, television and film programmes together.

3rd ed., 565 pp., 242 illus.

THE TECHNIQUE OF FILM ANIMATION

By John Halas and Roger Manvell

The aims and organization of making animated films on an industrial level. Shows the immense scope the medium offers.

4th ed., 360 pp., 247 illus.

THE TECHNIQUE OF FILM AND TELEVISION MAKE-UP

By Vincent J.-R. Kehoe

Intended primarily for the professional make-up artist, but the amateur will find invaluable its new ideas, advice and information.

3rd ed., 280 pp., 313 illus.

THE TECHNIQUE OF THE MOTION PICTURE CAMERA

By H. Mario Raimondo Souto

A wealth of information not only on camera design, but on the operation and maintenance of individual models.

3rd ed., 322 pp., 191 illus.

THE TECHNIQUE OF DOCUMENTARY FILM PRODUCTION

By W. Hugh Baddeley

How to plan, budget for and produce documentaries under present day conditions.

4th ed., 268 pp., 63 illus.

FOCAL BOOKS ON AMATEUR CINE

ALL-IN-ONE CINE BOOK

By Paul Petzold

Enables the non-technically minded beginner to get the most from his camera without fuss.

3rd *ed.*, 224 *pp.*, 234 *diag. and illus.*

CINE CRAFT

By J. D. Beal

Shows how groups of amateurs, children, or the lone worker can achieve successful films using a simple cine camera.

256 *pp.*, 292 *illus.*

HOW TO MAKE MOVIE MAGIC

By Julien Caunter

Here are all the ways and means to lift your films out of the run-of-the-mill.

348 *pp.*, 340 *illus.*

THE SUPER 8 FILM MAKER'S HANDBOOK

By Byron A. Matzkin

It gives special emphasis to the hardware in use and deals with cine cameras, lenses, film, related equipment and techniques.

320 *pp.*, 110 *photos*, 166 *diag.*

FOCAL AUDIO VISUAL BOOKS

VISUAL AIDS AND PHOTOGRAPHY IN EDUCATION

By M. J. Langford

A practical manual on the production of educationally sound visual aids by the working teacher.

350 *pp.*, 45 *photographs*, 660 *diag.*

TEACHING BY PROJECTION

By R. Stephen Judd

The theory in the early chapters prepares the ground for the detailed practical advice about using projection aids which follows.

168 *pp.*, 21 *diag.*

TEACHING WITH TAPE

By J. Graham Jones

It is a guide to many ways in which tape recording can help teachers and all who have to train the young.

2nd *enlarged ed.*, 176 *pp.*, 22 *diag.*

FUN WITH TAPE

By J. G. Staab

Covers a whole world of fun and usefulness; tape correspondence, the tape dialogue, the tape report and the tape interview.

248 *pp.*, 59 *diag.*

SLIDE TAPE AND DUAL PROJECTION

By Ray Beaumont-Craggs

For tape recording enthusiasts, photographers, photographic and amateur cine clubs, teachers, and sales and publicity personnel.

180 *pp.*, 89 *diag.*

COLOUR IN YOUR CAMERA

By Gösta Skoglund

A book of colour photos to show how to make colour photos, and it is concerned with the actual taking of the picture.

208 *pp.*, 202 *colour plates.*

FOCAL SOUNDBOOKS

THE ALL-IN-ONE TAPE RECORDER BOOK

By JOSEPH M. LLOYD

Everything that matters or is of interest, from first easy-to-understand principles to special recording techniques.

212 *pages*, 150 *diagrams.*

THE GRUNDIG BOOK

By FREDERICK PURVES

Recording procedure is described and illustrated fully, from the basic methods of recording to the techniques of "dubbing" and mixing.

216 *pages*, 90 *diagrams.*

THE DRAMATAPE GUIDE

By H. WOODMAN

How you can shape your play-readings into a presentation in sound. You don't need to be technically minded.

92 *pages*, 40 *diagrams.*

THE PHILIPS TAPE RECORDING BOOK

By FREDERICK PURVES

A comprehensive guide to the present range of Philips tape recorders, their operation and accessories.

216 *pages*, 142 *diagrams.*

SOUND: FACTS AND FIGURES

Compiled by JOHN BORWICK

All the data and know-how you need to get the best sound quality from discs, tape, radio and film.

172 *pages*, 183 *diagrams.*

COLLECTING GRAMOPHONE RECORDS

By E. T. BRYANT

An excellent guide that shows how to start a collection, choose the player, store and catalogue records.

160 *pages*, 40 *diagrams.*

MEDIA MANUALS AND RELATED FOCAL TITLES

BASIC TV STAGING

By GERALD MILLERSON

170 pages, 431 two-colour diagrams. Casebound and paperback.

TV CAMERA OPERATION

By GERALD MILLERSON

160 pages, 387 pages of two-colour diagrams. Casebound and paperback.

THE SMALL TV STUDIO

By ALAN BERMINGHAM, JOHN SYMONS, MICHAEL TALBOT SMITH and KENNETH ANGOLD-STEPHENS

152 pages, 72 pages two-colour illustrations. Paperback.

16 mm FILM CUTTING

By JOHN BURDER

144 pages, 64 pages two-colour illustrations. Paperback.

THE USE OF MICROPHONES

By ALEC NISBETT

168 pages, 172 two-colour illustrations. Casebound and paperback.

YOUR FILM AND THE LAB

By BERNARD HAPPÉ

160 pages, 362 two-colour illustrations. Casebound and paperback.

TV LIGHTING METHODS

By GERALD MILLERSON

192 pages, 112 photographs, 73 pages two-colour illustrations. Paperback.

TV SOUND OPERATIONS

By GLYN ALKIN

144 pages, 64 pages two-colour illustrations. Paperback.

LIBRARY OF FILM AND TELEVISION PRACTICE

THE WORK OF THE FILM DIRECTOR

By A. J. Reynertson

This book combines theory with a practical "on-the-set" approach to film making. It will add to anyone's appreciation of films by providing an understanding of film direction as a highly complex task.

260 *pp.*, 63 *photographs*, 11 *diag.*

THE WORK OF THE MOTION PICTURE CAMERAMAN

By Freddie Young and Paul Petzold

A description of the work of the film cameraman in a major film feature production. It describes his working environment, day-to-day routine and equipment.

248 *pp.*, 44 *photographs*, 124 *diag.*

THE WORK OF THE SCIENCE FILM MAKER

By Alex Strasser

The films studied here include any film of a scientific or technological character, whether made by a scientist, a professional film unit, a teacher or any other kind of film maker.

306 *pp.*, 125 *photographs*, 125 *diag.*

THE WORK OF THE INDUSTRIAL FILM MAKER

By John Burder

An industrial film can sell, train, convince, explain and instruct. It can be a first class investment. This book explains how and why.

256 *pp.*, 62 *photographs*

THE WORK OF THE TELEVISION JOURNALIST

By Robert Tyrrell

Television journalism is never the work of one man. It depends on a team of talents and skills. This book supplies the knowledge for the members to work as a unit.

180 *pp.*, 52 *diagrams and illustrations.*